THE COMPLEAT *Belly Dancer*

THE COMPLEAT

Belly Dancer

JULIE RUSSO MISHKIN AND

MARTA SCHILL

DOUBLEDAY & COMPANY, INC.

GARDEN CITY, NEW YORK

ISBN: 0-385-03556-x
Library of Congress Catalog Card Number 72–92407
Copyright © 1973 by Two Goats Incorporated

Printed in the United States of America
9   8   7   6

DEDICATED TO OUR SISTERS

CONTENTS

Contents

BELLY DANCING
FOR THE EVERYBODY

If you're bored, bloated, stooped, and draggy, grab your skimpiest work-out clothes and shake off those doldrums: The ancient wonders of belly dancing are yours for the twist of a hip!

What will belly dancing do for you and your body?

First of all, it will tone your entire musculature, resulting in a shapelier contour and improved posture. It will loosen up your spirits and your back-bone, letting the vertebrae uncoil into your natural serpentine state of spinal affairs.

One student's doctor verified that she had grown taller by ¾ of an inch after three months of belly-dance exercise. This was an extreme case of stiff back!

Another student swears her golf game improved fantastically because she was more agile with the twist at the Big Tee.

Several students have thrown away their confining elastic girdles and re-placed them with jingly coin belts after belly-roll workouts and rib lifts gave them a new outlook on the midriff scene.

9

The Compleat Belly Dancer

Those tight, rigid torso muscles respond to exercise and dance movement, letting the body become sinewy, flexible, and lithe. The rib cage lifts the abdominal muscles, creating a more youthful oval mound where the chubby pot belly used to hang.

Tensions that once accumulated like iron barnacles in the upper back and neck melt away. Arm movements become more graceful. (Quick: What's the most expressive thing you've done with *your* arms this week?)

How about the belly-dance student who claims she passed her driving test mainly because the inspector was so impressed with her graceful wrist action . . . said she looked so smooth and poised he was going to pass her, depite the fact that she had driven over the curb upon making a right turn.

And how about the husband of a student who swore his wife's belly dancing saved their marriage . . . mainly because she worked out all her tensions and found her voice had returned to its mellow pre-tension resonance.

Belly-dancing's rhythmic undulations will vitalize every part of the body as you stretch, twist, shimmy, and roll your way around this contemporized version of the ancient dance. Doctors acclaim it, recommending it even to sixty-year-old patients. While it may not actually take off pounds (that has to do with what you eat, too, you know!), it will help whittle away the useless, shapeless pouches and dreary paunches and help cure waistline hangovers.

Whether you want to keep fit to improve your golf game, to get back in shape after having a baby, to increase your bizazz! or to liven up your spare time, belly dancing will make you more at ease with your body and your self-image. It can lead only to liking your self more than before . . . back when you were bored, bloated, stooped, and draggy.

Tirelessly the lustful move
In gentle tremor eager limbs

MARTIAL

THE COMPLEAT *Belly Dancer*

One

SO YOU WANT TO BECOME A SENSUOUS BELLY DANCER

wherefores and whys

THE HIGH PRIESTESS

Belly dancing, the High Priestess in the world of female movement, is as new as she is ancient; as reverent as she is notorious.

The Priestess has been called a floozy in her day, but she has also mesmerized kings and honored the Gods.

From her origins as a vital participant in pagan ritual in the days of the Pharaohs, some 3,500 years ago, the belly dance came to the United States at the turn of the twentieth century. For decades, she contented herself with the often shadowy role of a show performance executed by questionably dark-haired beauties, always named as exotically as they were garbed. Hollywood loved her but understood her not. Ballerinas shunned her as the black shepherdess of the flock. Today, she is gathering thousands of devotees in such unlikely temples as YMCA gymnasiums, university campuses, recreation and community centers, and private dance studios throughout the nation. She has cleared her name, and dances on with new pride in an almost faddish revival of interest in the "authentic, reverent, ethnic art form."

SALOME'S SECRET

From whence slithered all those limber, voluptuous, and "foreign" devotees? Audiences in New York's plentiful Middle Eastern cabarets and night clubs, and in cities throughout the country, clapped, panted, and threw tips to countless Fatimas from Egypt, Sultanas and Salomes from Constantinople and other far-off desert harems.

The High Priestess drew a bevy of hard-working, quick-learning converts for, then as now, with the exception of a few true-blooded immigrants and authentic second-generation daughters, most Fatimas respond just as quickly when called by the less-enchanting sound of Jane or Margaret, being true Irish lasses or Jewish princesses by day.

Despite the less-than-sacred atmosphere of night clubs and cabarets, the Oriental Dance, as it is often called, survived and, truly, even blossomed. Back home, in the countries surrounding the sultry Mediterranean, stretching from Turkey to Morocco, the dance experienced a glittering revival as American and European tourists went looking for the real thing. The "real thing" in a Beirut night club is definitely a spin-off from the Yankee cabaret version of the ancient ethnic movements, but as with the other Wonders of the World, there's nothing like American enthusiasm to inspire the owners of tourist-drawing establishments. What was in danger of becoming buried with the rest of the old generation's backward ways was redeemed from the way of the veil and the harem, both of which institutions are not modern or Western enough for today's more sophisticated Middle Easterner.

THE BELLY AS MESSAGE

No amount of night-club choreography or questionable ethnic sequins could ever obliviate the true spirit of the Priestess. (The word sequin itself comes from the Arabic coins often attached to garments. They were not purple or pink, but were very shiny.)

Arabic dancing is still the ultimate in sensual womanly expression. Lest the Women's Liberation devotees misunderstand or develop mixed loyalties, let it be said that there is nothing unliberated about moving as a woman. The show girl may well be seen as a paid sex object. A woman having a good time within her body, sharing her delight in motor expression, cannot be exploited.

As a High Priestess, the Arabic belly dance is to striptease what the Persian carpet is to a shocking-pink nylon-shag throw rug; and to bottomless and topless bar performances as to the yellow-red-blue-green-flecked but still gray linoleum. What is it that is still enchanting? Anthropologists passed it off rather anatomically, categorizing it as "abdominal dancing." As such, it is found in the native dance of several "primitive cultures."

In the Middle East, credited by anthropologists as being the largest geographic area to utilize the stomach as dancer, music and self-expression have historically been wedded to dancing. Since the earliest days of mankind, when movement was more natural than speech, dancing in this region of the world has been the easiest and most popular form of communication. The Belly as Media. The Belly as Message.

Why the belly? In the first place, the belly is the center of birth and sexual movement. The place of the beginnings. And, as musicians and dancers in the Middle East often go on for hours on end, great physical exertion is required. Often, as the music grows more frenzied, the dancer is forced to stand in place and just shake the body and flutter the abdominal muscles in time to the music. When the French first saw the dance performed, they named it *danse du ventre* (dance of the stomach). It was in America that it was translated as belly dance after Little Egypt presented the form and the flutters for the first time in New York during the '30s.

INTER-ORIENTAL MAGIC

In the land of its origin, it was just dance. The Arabs called it Beledi, which means, simply, native dance or native rhythm. It is an alliterative coincidence that the Arabic word also sounds like belly. Oriental dance, Middle Eastern dance, or Arabic dance are some nice ethnic euphemisms for it. Just don't call it hootchie-kootch.

Oriental dancing derives from much more than Arabia proper. It encompasses Morocco, West Africa, Algiers, the African borderland of the Mediterranean through Syria, Iraq, Turkey, Persia, and even Greece and Northern India. The Arabs mingled with all the nations of the Near East, and their musical life had an international, inter-oriental character we call Arabian. When Islam unified the Middle East in the seventh century, the culture became homogenous.

In these lands, the passions of birth and life and love are woven into every

17

facet of the culture with a special earthy quality that transcends morality in the Western sense. Because of this, the Westerner has often misunderstood the dance, giving it his notoriety and striptease condescension. The music is highly emotional and very free rhythmically. Naturally, the dance, as a physical expression of that sensual, mystical music, is of the same stuff. There is magic in these parts of the world, and the music reflects thousands of regional customs, practices, and celebrations.

FLESH-COLORED MEMORIES

As much as belly dancing can be generalized in origin to the Middle East, it is fought over for definite national invention. The early Phoenicians did it; the ladies of the Pharaohs did it; the Turks claim it as theirs; the Egyptians point to their ancient wall paintings, sculpture, and artifacts to prove it was truly theirs. The North African Berbers probably don't care, but many ethnomusicologists lay the source in their deserts. And there are differences from country to country. Throughout the classical Arabic world, where women are bound by the Islam code to stay covered from toe to fingertip, dancers wore completely covering robes, robes over veils over baggy trousers. In Egypt today, on a decree issued as a result of the 1952 revolution, cabaret dancers are required to be completely dressed. Many get around this prohibition by wearing flesh-colored body stockings under their costumes.

North African tribal women—whose claim to the dance stems from age-old folk dances where women shuffled—the stories say, turned to dancing in the market place in hopes of winning the favors of passers-by sufficiently to get a few gold coins tossed at their feet. The coins were taken home and sewn onto a belt or girdle, which was worn whenever the hopeful, but poor, girl danced. Eventually, she earned enough coins with her dancing to represent a sizable dowry. Ironically, once she married she would never dance again, save for her husband. She had danced to insure herself a respectable life.

It is also told that the belly dance was performed by helpful village women as another sister was giving birth to a child. The dance served as a rhythmic, soothing reminder to the woman in labor to use her abdominal muscles to aide the birth process.

Some tales come right out of history. The famous Theodora is said to have been a featured belly dancer in a circus before she became Empress of Byzantium. And then, there are all those stories about slave girls being forced to dance in some strange, exotic land far from home, longing all the time for her handsome Nordic lover back on the fjords.

18

CREAKING WESTERNERS

It may be because the polkas, square dances, and minuets of Western man lack the earthy, unifying sensuality of Middle Eastern dance that the Yankee has been so beguiled by the Priestess. Western man and woman have done a good job of separating themselves from their bodies, or denying much of the body in self-expression. He and she move only when they have to: in work, a righteous use of the body; in soul and communication, a stiff flop. In desperate creaking throngs, the Westerner counts on boring tedium of exercise without soul to attempt to keep in shape. Many turn to the more aggressive physical expressions in athletics and sports. Women go to figure salons where the buttocks and calves are treated as parts of a machine. The Westerner rarely lets himself express ecstasy or longing in a spontaneous burst of flapping arms or poignant reaching out. He is sadly atrophied; separated from the body soul.

How much more complete and intense the response of more primitive man, whose unburdened mind offered so little resistance to every stimulus. Simpler folk responded to the native drum beat with total abandon. Therapy was party time. The movements of sexual domain—conception and giving birth—were considered natural as any other. Pelvic movement and undulation was not a matter of sensation and pleasure, but of life and unity with nature.

Western man has been turning increasingly to the East for extra-curricular spiritual knowledge. Now, he turns to the Middle East for rhythmic reinforcement. But there is much to learn—and unlearn, in both instances.

A course on belly dancing must include preparatory exercises to limber up, stretch, and condition the body and bring it back to a more natural ability to express. Belly dancing is nothing more than very natural movement. Much of its appeal lies in its more sensual, more earthy nature. The West is truly learning to contemplate—and appreciate—its navel.

RED-BLOODED AMERICAN UNDULATIONS

It is really no surprise that the excitement of ethnic music, the sensual response it evokes, have been stirring interest at a rising rate within the last year or two. Scores of red-blooded American girls have penetrated the mystique of the belly dance and sought out instruction from professionals, or retired professionals, and spent hours at ringside seats in Middle Eastern clubs to try to learn another new step to practice at home.

Thousands of American women have started rolling their bellies and perfecting the snakelike undulations. They come for instruction for many reasons: to get back into shape after having a baby; to fulfill a secret alter-ego image; to express their total nature, including their sexuality, without losing any dignity or grace; to enhance their sex appeal; to entertain a bored husband; or just to have fun.

They come in all sizes, all shapes, all ages. Plumpies come to slim up, discovering that the exercises do miracles to tone up those loose muscles. Slender women (skinny, in fact, by Middle Eastern standards) become voluptuous, if only through loosening up enough to add round movements to their straight frames.

Some, a small minority, discover they possess a natural knack for the art, and go on to join the increasing ranks of professionals who perform in clubs and at thousands of more lucrative private-party engagements. And because the Oriental dance has earned back its respectability (or is it that the Puritanical attitude toward the body has enlarged considerably in the last few years?) an entire new breed of cabaret dancers is making its debut, drawing an enthusiastic new breed of aficionados. Rock musicians are becoming fascinated with the Oud, the Dumbeki, and the Saz. Any would-be belly dancer is invited to more parties than any calendar would allow for. The muse is with us, wearing finger cymbals and a veil . . . and more than likely, a head of store-bought Egyptian hair.

THE BUG AND YOU

And now there is you. Whatever your reasons for pursuing the High Priestess and her secret lore, there is something herein to enrich your awareness. If you don't have a particular motive in mind, let us suggest a few reliable ones. They may all apply.

1. You want to tone your muscles, improve your posture, develop more balance and grace in all your movements, increase your stamina, and perhaps decrease your girth and width. Belly dancing is one of the best all-around body improvers you'll ever find.

2. You want to give a private surprise recital for your man's birthday, or your anniversary, or just for the cultural shock of it all.

3. The dancing bug has bitten you—ballet is too rigid, jazz is too intellectual, the cha-cha-cha is dead. The belly dance is a supremely expressive way to move.

4. You always wished you were a Persian courtesan, a Theda Bara, or tantalizing gypsy. There is no mode of female adornment more befitting any such vision as those worn for belly dancing . . . in fact, take a look at any high-fashion magazine. Add a few movements and the right attitudes, and turn your mod wardrobe into a meaningful total environment.

5. The haunting, insistent rhythms of the Middle East have caught your soul. Yes, a dancer is the visual interpretation of all that vital improvisation.

6. You are sure you were a harem dancer in a former incarnation, and want to bring your past lives up to date.

7. You want to be able to tell the girls you've got to go home and practice belly dancing, leaving them to continue knitting.

8. You and your body and your soul are dangerously out of touch.

Whatever your reason for calling on the Ancient Lady, whether you call her Belly or Arabic or Beledi or Oriental, she responds only to the desire to dance. She will like you all the more if you're a bit on the plump side; give you extra grace and dimension if you are over thirty (even a professional well within her forties can mesmerize her audiences).

She'll set your body moving in an entirely new way—every part of you will move on its own, rotating or wiggling as though detached from the rest. The hands, legs, breasts, and, of course, the belly will say things you never even heard before. The Lady will mostly make herself felt in your hips, and of course, it would be just too cute to mention that she was the first and most literal of the hippies.

She and you may not save a marriage, bring you fame and fortune or complete happiness, but she can bring you back to your body, bring your body back to meaningful expression, and round out your cabaret universe.

Two

BEFORE YOU BEGIN
the very essentials

THE BASIC BELLY-DANCE POSITION

A body can only move so many ways . . . can only bend and undulate along so many curves. Just because you have been walking around like a stiff board these past few years doesn't mean you can't loosen up and add some space-swinging curves to your body's repertory.

Belly dancing is a matter of engineering. If you think it is just the tummy that sways around, you won't be moving much at all. The way you stand, your use of weight change, your understanding of your own center of gravity . . . and USING those joints and bendable places to give you more freedom of movement all go into play.

Just to prove to yourself how much engineering adds to your movability

. . . try this. Remember the old twist? Stand straight (well, slump your shoulders if that's what you've been doing anyway) and twist that derriere. Now, bend your knees as though you were about to start sitting down. Now twist a few sweeps with your derriere. Get the difference? You have engineered your body into a posture that allows for much more freedom of movement in the hips—and the belly.

The look of belly dancing is one which is set-up to provide the most freedom of movement. You can't disengage the hips from the torso, but you can master a few basic engineering techniques that will start you moving and undulating right away.

So, the first and most important thing a belly dancer must learn is how to stand, how to hold herself, how to distribute her weight, how to make gravity work for her.

Throughout the book, you will be asked to "Assume Basic Position." This, then, is the foundation for all your movements.

1. Knees slightly bent. (Tiring at first, until you have strengthened leg muscles.)
2. Weight on heels. (Gives you backward emphasis and frees hips.)
3. Rib cage up. (A puppeteer's string is pulling it up from above.)
4. Shoulders down and relaxed (not hunched up or pulled back *a la militaire*).
5. Abdominal muscles relaxed. (Let it all hang out.)

Visual images help: A puppeteer's string is attached to your sternum (right between the breasts on the rib cage), pulling from above to give you a good lift.

A slender pole runs plumb from the top of the head to the ground. At times this pole coincides with the spinal column. Usually, it becomes an imaginary center of gravity around which all movements revolve, undulate, and bend.

An invisible chair is always right behind you (perhaps one of those stump stools used on the farm by maidens milking the cows). You are often in a position to just about sit back on it.

Your feet are always ready to sift sand or work a little hole in the earth. A belly dancer's toes are her earthy contact.

Three

STRETCH, BEND, AND TWIST
conditioning exercises

WARMING UP AND GETTING IN SHAPE

There's no magical, instant formula for learning any kind of body movement. It still takes a well-oiled set of joints and muscles that are capable of smooth response and stamina. But no scrawny weakling could ever possess a sensuous body—within or without the form of dance—until, that is, it is given a chance.

The following set of exercises will give you just that . . . a second chance to bring you and your body closer together. There are countless exercises in the world of body-improvement. We have selected those that best suit the needs of the belly dancer. Many are virtually dance steps themselves. There are several fringe benefits awaiting the woman who spends just ten minutes a day with these stretches and toners. Posture and carriage will be enhanced; the bosom will achieve a firmer line; the belly muscles will get toned up; walking up and down stairs will be a breeze. The tensions which love to accumulate like barnacles in the neck and back will be exorcized. All the things your body can do for you will be done fuller, easier, more enjoyably.

You'll want music to exercise and dance to. An extended-play 45-rpm record, written and arranged specially for readers of this book, is available by mail. (See information at the end of the book.) This compact record includes a highly rhythmic Beledi, or moderately fast number; and, on the other side, a slow snake dance taxim and Tcheftetelli rhythm and drum solo. It is specifically designed to turn you on . . . to make movements easy and natural.

Of course, you may also visit a local record store and purchase a long-playing album . . . but listen to it first. Avoid the heavily instrumentalized Egyptian music. It is too undefined for most new dancers. We recommend two excellent recordings:

"The Fez"—a recently waxed album recorded live at an Arabic club in Los Angeles, featuring Maroun Saba and Abboud Abdel Al and his orchestra. One side is a complete and diversified belly dancers' routine now being used by professionals who work without live musicians, and is available nationally. (Fez Records, 1972)

or

"An Evening at the Seventh Veil," also recorded live at a club, featuring Armenian musicians (SVS-1001) and available nationally.

If worst comes to worst and there is no way for you to get a record, or you just can't wait for the mail-order record, get someone to play the piano . . . "Hava Nagila," that well-known Israeli-Jewish folk song, makes for a good fast dance; "Miserlou" or "Caravan" are good for slow movements. You might even find an acceptable "Muzak" recording containing suitable bolero or other exotic rhythms to work with until you get the real thing.

Try each exercise according to directions. Go easy with yourself the first few sessions. Enjoy yourself, while you're at it. Put on the record and bounce in time to the beat. After the initial grunts and groans periods, you'll look forward to your own ten-minute body sessions. Always do your exercises before moving on to the dance steps. Your muscles will reward you for the increased circulatory flow and general lubricating warm-up you'll be giving them by responding more to your dance attempts.

If you feel achy the second day, keep doing the exercises anyway . . . at your own pace. The worst thing you can do for a muscle ache is to limp.

It is sending you the message that you have not used it enough in the past and would greatly appreciate a continued workout until it is back to its natural state of development.

Once you have done the exercises for a week or so, the pattern will become automatic to you. You might also find that any excuses about being too busy are best checked by becoming sneaky with your exercises—sneak in a few while you're boiling potatoes; as you're gabbing on the phone; invite a few friends to join you.

Read the directions for each exercise before you begin. Refer to the illustrations. Check yourself out with a mirror. Start stretching. . . .

CONDITIONING STRETCHES AND LOOSENERS

OVERHEAD STRETCH

LOVELY PULL FROM HEAD TO TOE

1. Stand tall.
2. Wrap right hand around left wrist.
3. Stretch—pulling left arm up. You should feel pull in waist.
4. Change hands—pull right arm up.
5. Repeat, alternating hand hold, 4 times.

Stretch—pulling left arm up. You should feel pull in waist.

SIDE-TO-SIDE STRETCH BEND

to make you ooh! and ah!

1. Right hand grasps left wrist.
2. Pulling left arm straight over head in line with ear, bend at waist as far as possible toward right side.
3. Straighten up. Change hands. Repeat, alternating sides, 4 times.

Pulling left arm straight over head in line with ear, bend at waist as far as possible toward right side.

Straighten up. Change hands. Repeat, alternating sides, 4 times.

CIRCLE BOUNCE STRETCH

develops balance, limberness . . .
a big circle of you.

PART 1

1. Drop forward, flop hands to floor. Bounce 8 times . . . like a rag doll.
2. Stand upright. Raise left hand overhead. Right hand on right hip. Reach and bend straight over to right, bending and stretching from waist. Bounce 8 times.

29

3. Stand straight. Hands on both hips, elbows bent. Lean backward from bent and lowered knees. Bounce 8 times. Bend as far as possible, as in limbo dancing.

4. Stand upright. Raise right hand overhead. Left hand on left hip. Reach and bend straight over to left, bending and stretching from waist. Bounce 8 times.

YOU HAVE NOW BENT AND STRETCHED YOUR WAY AROUND A FULL CIRCLE; FRONT, BACK, AND BOTH SIDES. CONTINUE WITH THIS EXERCISE TO DEVELOP A SINGLE, SMOOTH CIRCULAR MOVEMENT . . . ONE OF THE KEYS TO BELLY DANCING.

Reach and bend straight over to left, bending and stretching from waist. Bounce 8 times.

CIRCLE STRETCH

PART II

1. Using previous pattern—forward, side, backward, side—bouncing only 4 times in each direction.
2. Repeat again, bouncing only twice in each direction.
3. THE GRAND FINALE—Make just ONE bounce in each direction, completing circle twice. Be sure to stand upright between each directional bend.

FLOOR STRETCHES

reaching for a better body

SIT ON FLOOR . . . LEGS SPREAD IN V. Keep your back straight as possible. While doing this exercise, let your hands move gracefully . . . time to start dancing is right now.

TOUCHING TOES

1. Reach both hands over head. Bend to touch toes or grasp ankles with both hands. Try to lower head to touch knee.

Reach both hands over head. Bend to touch toes or grasp ankles with both hands. Try to lower head to touch knee.

2. Sit upright, gracefully crossing arms and hands toward right.

3. Bend to touch right toe, attempting to lower head to knee.

Repeat 4 times, alternating side to side. THEN . . .

TOUCH THE GROUND

1. With legs still spread, reach forward toward floor, bending from hips. As you pull forward, attempt to pull head to floor. This will require considerable practice so don't worry if you don't make contact. The important thing is to make the attempt.

Now, let's combine these two stretches and make a . . .

TOE-TO-TOE SWING

From sitting upright position (legs still spread), arms overhead, bend to left toe, swing to center, then to right toe, return to straight sitting position. You are making a U-shaped pattern.

THE ELBOW STRETCH

1. Still sitting on floor with legs spread, clasp hands behind head, pulling back on elbows to make as straight a line with your arms as possible.

2. Reach to left side, trying to touch floor with left elbow. Work toward bending straight to side, but we all know we at first will bend at an angle more toward the knee.

THE ELBOW STRETCH

Indian Fashion

1. Sitting on floor place soles of feet together.

2. Place hands on respective ankles with elbows over knees. Push down with arms. (That ouch means it's working . . . stretching out the legs, increasing your "spread," generally doing great things for a belly dancer's most important tools, the knees.)

3. Now, place hands behind head as in former exercise. With feet still touching, sole-to-sole, bend sideways to touch elbows to floor, first at left, then at right.

YOU SHOULD NOW FEEL LOOSE, FLEXIBLE, STRETCHED, AND READY TO GO DANCING. BEGIN EVERY WORKOUT SESSION WITH THESE EXERCISES. THEY GET EASIER AS YOU GO ALONG . . . WITHIN A WEEK YOU WILL ACTUALLY LOOK FORWARD TO DOING THEM. NOTHING WORKS OUT THE TENSIONS AND CRIMP-INGS OF EVERYDAY LIFE QUITE SO WELL.

THE BACK-ROLL BRIDGE

works your spine into snaky flexibility

1. Lie on floor, knees bent, feet flat. Arms relaxed at sides. Head straight.
2. Lift torso up off floor so a slanted line is formed from knees to head.
3. S-L-O-W-L-Y now, start lowering your spine to the floor, beginning at the neck. Use your legs and feet for strength and anchoring.

NOTE: As you uncurl through the small of your back, tuck in the pelvis. Make sure each part of the back touches the floor . . . keep going through to the "tailbone." Attempt to roll each single vertebrae one at a time.
4. Relax. Pushing with feet, flatten small of back again. Release.

36

Lift torso up off floor so a slanted line is formed from knees to head.

S-L-O-W-L-Y now, start lowering your spine to the floor, beginning at the neck. Use your legs and feet for strength and anchoring.

THE GARBO TWIST

Here's a great twister . . . gives your upper half an angle on flexibility while your neck and head get a chance to stretch into a haughty sensuality.

1. Stand upright. Right elbow behind ribs, left elbow in front. Using right arm only, pull upper torso into a sideways twist, turning toward right. Do not move hips. Let left side be pulled around to front.

2. Simultaneously, turn head to left, stretching at chin. Hold chin parallel to shoulder . . . feeling that great neck-shaping pull.

3. Return to center position. Now, pull left elbow back to bring torso into side twist. Head turns to right shoulder. Do not let head tilt—merely stretch and revolve it into correct position.

ALONE BUT NOT LONELY—
THE ISOLATION EXERCISES

If the first key to belly dancing is to be loose and flexible, the second key is to be able to utilize isolation. Isolation means moving one part of the body (such as the rib cage) while the rest of the body holds still; or moving one part of the body one way while another (say the hips) moves all on its own. Mastering isolation is not as hard as it may seem. Most of us are never called upon to move just one part of our body. Most things get done very well with a whole lunge, or a whole shake. These exercises will help your brain center learn the right messages to send, for instance, to just the ribs, or just the hips, while sending orders to the neighboring anatomy to hold still. We know that the thigh bone is connected to the hip bone and on and on . . . but the connection is controlled through muscles, and we can teach our muscles to move in solo fashion. When you first try to send such a message, your switchboard is going to react with confusion. For some, isolated movements come easily. For others, not a damn thing will budge at first. Don't give up. We haven't seen a student yet who hasn't unraveled the code in a few patient attempts. A mirror is your best friend at times like these. If you work with another person, you have two best friends, for there's nothing like a hand holding still the parts you don't want to move while you go to work on the part you *do*.

AS EASY AS BREATHING IN AND OUT
AND UP AND DOWN AND ALL AROUND

Another key—moving the rib cage. Without learning to isolate the rib cage, the snake becomes a stiff piece of pipe. Most of us have long hence allowed our rib cages to become frozen . . . ever hear of the intercostal muscles? They are a web of little muscle strands that connect each rib to the other. After a few years of slumping, the intercostals have become shrunken and atrophied. But all is not lost—they are only too eager to become revived and vital again. By giving them this second chance, your entire posture, dancing or not, will be given an amazing uplift. The bosom is enhanced (the breast is getting a virtually free ride on those crumpled muscles: throw away your padding, but not necessarily your bra) and the abdomen molds back into a feminine oval, uplifted into a younger shape rather than forced into a lopsided tuck. The belly, after all, does not begin at the waist. It extends from the rib cage to the pelvic floor. Working on reviving the natural uplift is like tightening up the skin of a drum . . . everything gets a higher tone. Your viscera—all those invisible organs inside—will prosper for the uplift too.

DEEP-BREATHING LIFT

1. If you think your rib cage can't move an inch, just try this startling demonstration of just how much movability you do possess even now.

    a. Stand straight

    b. Take three deep breaths . . . inhale, letting the ribs expand to their fullest. Exhale, letting them drop back down.

    c. Now—make the same lifting motion, but do not take in any air. You should see your ribs moving just as much as when you were breathing. (Naturally, you will want to breathe again as soon as you have proven this to yourself.)

THE LONELY RIB CAGE

shake up the bird, but keep the tree trunk straight

1. Stand upright, arms bent, hands on hips.

2. Pretend your rib cage is resting on a silver platter . . . and the silver platter is anchored onto a pedestal.

3. Push the rib cage to the right. Now push it to the left.

4. THINGS NOT TO MOVE—the hips, the legs, the shoulders, the head. There will be reflex movement . . . it really is connected, if by nothing less than skin, you know. But try to minimize ACTIVE movement . . . initiated movement is all in the rib cage. Don't cheat by LEANING side-to-side.

Push the rib cage to the right. Now push it to the left.

5. Start moving slowly from side to side . . . big, long, slow pushes. As you limber up, try a few fast dashes from side to side.

6. It is sometimes easier to get the message by holding arms out to the sides at shoulder level. If you do this, be careful not to cheat by pulling arms or playing airplane.

THE CANADIAN AIR FORCE RIB LIFT

Here's a foolproof way to start getting messages to JUST your rib cage . . . developed by the belly dancer's unexpected ally, the Canadian Air Force.

1. Lie flat on the floor . . . a Persian carpet makes an appropriate and comfortable cushion for this movement.

2. Arms at side, upper arm almost tucked under sides of back.

3. Lift ONLY rib cage as high off floor as possible. Return to floor. Repeat.

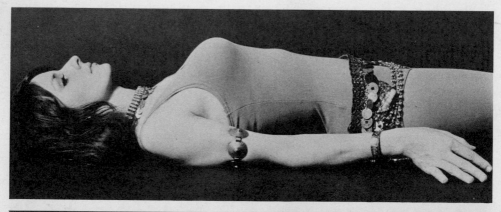

THE DIAMOND ROLL

This requires more effort than breathing in-and-out . . . you are going to extend your rib cage movability to include side-to-side as well as in-and-out and up-and-down. All that pushing and pulling results in quite a side show in the belly muscles . . . and is one of those "Belly-dancer Look" movements.

1. Stand upright. Keep shoulders down and relaxed. Try not to move hips.

2. Start tracing an imaginary diamond, first working to the four corners, then rounding it off into an egg-shaped oval roll.

    a. Start by pushing the rib cage over to the left side.

    b. Inhale as you push up to the top point of the diamond.

c. Now, down to the right side of your diamond.

d. Exhaling, move on to the bottom center point of the dia-mond.

CLUE: Hold hand on hips. As you INHALE to raise the rib cage up, push down with hands on pelvis bones. As you exhale to allow rib cage to drop down, relax pressure of hands.

THE 10 O'CLOCK ROLL

a super Belly-Dance Key

1. Stand upright. Imagine a clockface. Your head is at 12 o'clock. Facing toward the 9, lift the rib cage to 10 o'clock (forward and up). KEEP SHOULDERS DOWN. Continue tracing the clock with an imaginary point on your sternum.

2. Lift (with a heave) the rib cage up to 12 o'clock, then let it fall backward down through 1, 2, 3, 4, 5, and 6 (at 6, you will be sunken). From 6 on it's lift and thrust back (and ever so roundly) to 10, where you can start again.

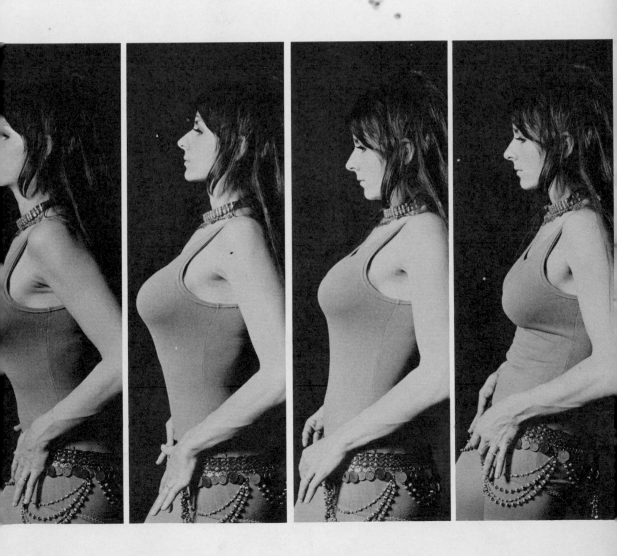

THE EXOTIC HEAD

You've seen this one . . . maybe even played around with it. It appears in the dances of many countries, primarily India and Egypt. It, too, requires patience rather than hard work. If you start working on it early in your preparation, it will appear one day to add a mysterious, haunting touch to your movements. It may interest you to know that you can move your head without moving a muscle in the neck. At first you will move your neck, and the effect is Turkey-ish. Work for a relaxed neck. (CLUE: The head is connected to the spine at the occipital joint, high up the nape of the neck.)

EAVESDROPPING

Stand in a doorway. Place palms of hands on sides of door. Push toward door. Now, try to bend ear over to each side.

THUMBS UP

Make fist of hands. Bend elbows, chicken fashion, placing little-finger side of fist on each collarbone. Thumbs up. Now, try to push head side to side so that the cheek-jaw touches the thumbs.

THE INDIAN SQUARE DANCE FOR HEAD

1. Working before a mirror, raise both arms above head. Hold hands high, loose and graceful, touching back-to-back (less corny than the oft-seen palm-to-palm pyramid).

2. Attempt to move neck side to side.

3. Now, make the four points of a square . . . head front right, head back right, head back left, head front left.

4. Work off the edges and make a circle with the head.

CARRY THOSE HIPS SWING

1. Bend knees. Tuck in derriere. Weight on heels. This position is another Belly-Dancer Key . . . here's why: Pretend your hips are a pendulum.

2. Push hips side to side . . . absorbing all movement below waist. (The old book-on-the-head routine works well here to remind you to do all your moving with your bottom half.)

3. The trick is in the knees . . . pushing and adjusting and compensating so that there is no up-and-down movement. Equality of movement, equal swing, equal bend, is what you are after.

YOUR THIGHS AND KNEES ARE GOING TO GET FRINGE BENEFITS FROM THIS EX-ERCISE. THE MORE YOU BEND YOUR KNEES, THE MORE YOUR LEGS MUST WORK TO CARRY THOSE HIPS.

Most of us might as well be welded together—especially in the shoulders. Let's take the bonds of unwanted togetherness away and see how much more relaxed and attractive all our movements are.

THE TURTLE SCRUNCH

how the models get the long-necked look

1. Sit or stand. Hunch your shoulders up and scrunch your neck down so that it almost disappears . . . just like a turtle pulling a fast retreat.

2. Emerge as a swan—pull your neck up and lower your shoulders. Push shoulders down as if a heavy weight is resting on each.

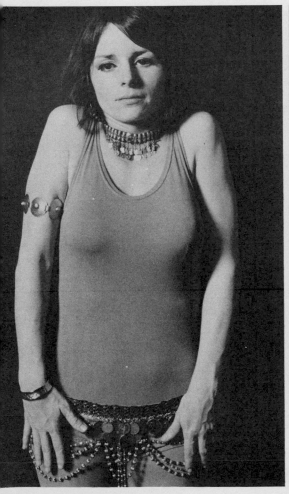 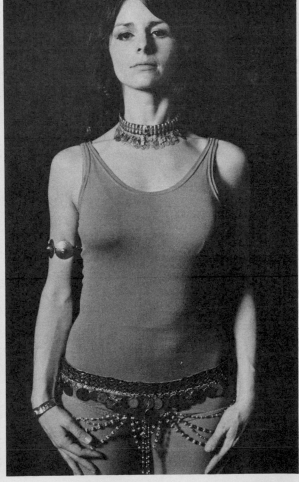

NECK ROLL

a toner and relaxer

1. Stand. Drop head forward so chin touches chest. (Feel that great pull? You bet it's working!) Now, with a relaxed neck . . .
2. Slowly rotate head to one side.

3. Let head roll backward. (Open mouth for ease.)
4. Continue letting it roll to other side, then return to center. Continue and reverse.

SHOULDER SHRUG

1. Stand. Lift right shoulder as high as you can—straight up.
2. Let shoulder fall as though the puppeteer's string has been suddenly released. The arm just rides along . . . all INITIATED movement is from shoulder.
3. Repeat with left shoulder.
4. Continue, alternating shoulders.

THE WINGS

1. Stand. Bring both shoulders as far forward as possible. (Just the shoul-

ders now . . . let the arms ride along . . . but keep the head and upper torso in place.)

2. Bring shoulders as far back as possible.
3. Repeat, alternating, 4 times.

CARROUSEL

1. Bring both shoulders around in a circle.
2. Bring shoulders up; pull as far backward as possible.

3. In continuing circular motion, push shoulders forward and back up.

4. Reverse, going forward.

THE PISTON VAMP

1. Let right shoulder move in a forward circle.

2. As right shoulder is up, left shoulder is down. (As right shoulder is back, left shoulder is forward.) Work on making a vampy, smooth swivel movement.

DANCER'S CLUE: As each shoulder moves forward, tilt head slightly to suggest contact with chin. This is a suggestion only . . . chin and shoulder do not touch.

THE BELLY FLOP

gets the vital muscles in shape

1. Stand. Push abdominal muscles out, expanding the belly. Just let the belly hang way out.

2. Exhale completely as you attempt to push the belly out even further.

3. Now, suck in your breath and pull those belly muscles in as far as you can, as if they were being pulled by strings attached to the spine.

4. Repeat, letting belly out and sucking it in.

NOTE: You will soon be able to do these expansion-contraction movements independent of your breathing. Play around with this exercise and you might find yourself belly dancing!

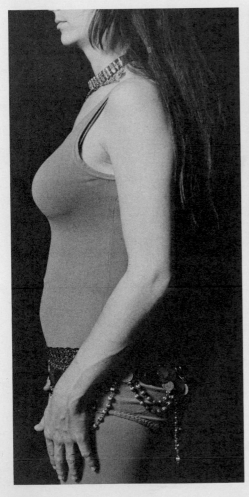 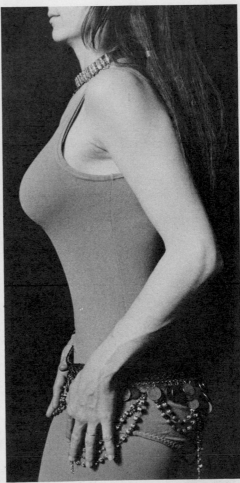

Four

STEPS, MOVEMENTS, AND SHAKES
the components

BASIC DANCE MOVEMENTS

No body learns to dance by exercise alone. But, as with any physical skill, the more you get your body in shape—free from old tensions and rigidities, stretched, and more under your conscious control—the more you will be able to lead your body into dance movement and self-expression.

You will discover that your approach to learning movements and steps is greatly enhanced—oiled, so to speak—if you start each practice session with the conditioning and isolation exercises.

Each week, your body will be more receptive to executing the belly-dance movements. Don't expect too much the first time or two . . . your body and mind are learning to deliver new messages to muscles that have probably been just barely surviving.

Work in front of a mirror . . . wear something that bares your belly so you can see the effects of your movements.

The Compleat Belly Dancer

The following chapter introduces to you the basic movements of belly dancing, and shows you how to understand the engineering and construction of several combination patterns and steps. Some will require more practice than others. (You can practice for a year and still want more smoothness, more control.) But for the enthusiastic novice who wants to start dancing right away, these movements will be usable with a minimum of practice. Since some bodies naturally pick up movements more easily than others, don't give up if it all seems impossible at first. And relax . . . that's more important than any exercise. RELAX. You're in this to enjoy yourself, as well as to accomplish something. You have nothing to prove to anyone . . . it's just you and your body, rediscovering how great it feels to move freely . . . and sensuously.

LEARNING PLAN

1. Warm up with your exercises. Spend about 10–15 minutes stretching, bending, twisting, etc.

2. Work on one or two new movements a day until you have covered the entire set.

3. You will be introduced to a dance-instruction system called the Belly-Dance Master. The Dance Master will be presented in two sections, each including basic movements and variations. Work out the patterns specified as soon as you feel even a little comfortable with the steps.

4. Each day, add to your practice repertoire. Work with a mirror. Check your image with the photographs and drawings in the book.

5. At first, wear a practice uniform—pants loose and low at the hips, a top that bares the midriff (just tie up a blouse); or a bikini.

6. No one learns to dance without dancing. Once you have the hang of a few patterns, tuck in your veil and start dancing . . . just for fun. Shut your eyes, be gentle with yourself and let your body express what your body is feeling.

THE BASIC MOVEMENTS YOU WILL LEARN
ARE:

A. Side-to-Side Sways
B. "Figure 8" Sways
C. Basic Lift Steps
D. Hip Lifts
E. Hip/Lower Torso Circles
F. Shimmies

SIDE-TO-SIDE SWAYS

the mesmerizers

Willowy, undulating sways with the hips getting a free ride on hard-working legs; an engineered weight-shift hip rock.

BREAKING IT DOWN

1. Assume Basic Position (knees slightly bent, belly relaxed, ribs held high, arms out at shoulder height, shoulders relaxed and down).
2. Shift weight to left foot.
3. Pushing with ball of left foot, shift back to right. Continue shifting weight from side to side until you are rocking in a supple sway.
4. NOW . . . as you are shifting from side to side, let the hips lead. When weight is assumed by right foot, hip rolls over and extends sideways, as if you were holding schoolbooks on the hip contour. Push with right leg, raising right hip slightly, and shift weight over to left foot, riding the hips back over the left side.
5. Work arms in push-and-pull counter movement to hip sway.

NOTES

1. Your weight is on the foot beneath the accented hip.
2. Let the hip fall to the side in a delayed action for even more undulation.
3. The hips move in a fall and rise because of the engineering of the leg push helping you shift weight.

Assume Basic Position (knees slightly bent, belly relaxed, ribs held high, arms out at shoulder height, shoulders relaxed and down).

Shift weight to left foot.

Pushing with ball of left foot, shift back to right. Continue shifting weight from side to side until you are rocking in a supple sway.

UNDERSTANDING IT

To limber up and strengthen the ankles and feet, and to grasp the feeling of using the feet to roll and push you into a smooth sway, practice this simple exercise.

THE FOOT ROLL

1. Right foot: Rolling from the ankle, press little toe only onto floor. Roll around to big toe, spreading all toes on the floor. Continue the circle along the arch side of the foot, around to the heel, then back to the little toe. Repeat with left foot.
2. Reverse direction of circle. Start with big toe, roll and spread around to the little toe, around the outside, heel, arch side, and back to the big toe.
3. CLUE: As you work your feet, alternating the exercise between right and left, notice how the knees adjust and move to allow the action. This is the "trick" to carrying those hips as they sway from side to side. The more you bend your knees, the more this motion will be emphasized.

HIP-STICK

This simple exercise demonstrates how the bending and straightening of the leg and foot will lift your hip for more undulation.

1. Assume Basic Position. Knees bent.
2. Keeping feet in position, lift onto ball of left foot.
3. Straighten knee of left leg, pushing hip upward toward shoulder.
4. Repeat with right. Continue, alternating.

DANCING WITH SIDE-TO-SIDE SWAYS

1. By varying the bend in your knees, you add improvisational dimensions to this very basic step. Try a teeter-totter sway: Bend down for one side of the sway, then back up for the other. Or, bend down for a set of sways, then raise up to tippy-toes for some more.
2. Vary the timing: Do one slow, extended, and virtually anguished sway; then thrust in a few more rapid swings.
3. Add a brush step. As your weight goes to the right foot, push the left to the side as if you were flicking away an intruding beetle . . . this sideways brush-kick adds more force to the movement, so be careful not to make it bouncy. Absorb the push in your hips.

MAKING IT GREAT

1. Work on minimizing the movement in your rib cage and shoulders. Practice with a book on your head to gain smoothness.

2. Later, when you have mastered the isolation and can control the movement from the hips down, you can get your back muscles, rib cage, and shoulders moving in opposition to the hips . . . a counter pull similar to swimming movements that adds the art of restraint to your sway and produces a sinuous, serpentine totality.

"FIGURE 8" SWAYS

the twisters

A very usable movement that involves a side-to-side and back-and-fro twist and sway. Produces fascinating side effects in the belly muscles. May be done with large, sweeping motions or very subtly, in standing or kneeling position.

BREAKING IT DOWN

1. Assume Basic Position. The more you bend your knees, the more movement you will get.

2. Bring your right hip back as far as it can go.

3. Swing the right hip as far forward as it can go, as if it were a swinging door.

4. You will notice that as your right hip swings forward the left hip will have swung backward.

5. Slide your weight, now on your right hip, back through your body until weight is resting on left hip in back. Now swing your left hip forward. Repeat weight shift.

CLUE: Imagine you are tracing a figure 8 with your hips. The right hip traces one half of the 8, the left traces the other.

Using your legs to engineer the weight transfer, concentrate on the diagonal line that connects the two sides. This is the crucial part of the movement, for the diagonal crossover line is where smoothness is achieved.

NOTE: Another step—the Half Moon—is similar to a reverse Figure 8, in which hips move from front to back.

MAKING IT GREAT

1. Minimize the movement from the rib cage up. Try to achieve a twist in the hips and legs only.

2. Vary the movement—make it small and subtle. Get down on your knees and do it. Bend your knees more and swing those doors around with a smooth fervor.

3. To make it a more controlled movement, practice it like this:

Bend knees, but tuck in derriere. As you now enact the Figure 8, it will pull on your belly muscles even more.

Now, get down on your knees and, with derriere still tucked under, repeat.

When standing, *do not* attempt this step in a fixed position—it will be jerky and "cut off" at every turn. Learn to pivot gracefully on the toe that brings the hip around. If it looks strange and "pigeon-toed," you're doing it right! Your long skirt (when dancing) will cover those hard-working feet —and your torso will appear to be almost magically floating in a graceful Figure 8.

THE BASIC LIFT STEP

the movers

THE BASIC LIFT STEP

When a village woman heard the insistent rhythms of the drummer, her first inclination was to mark time with her feet. Since she was looser and freer moving than her civilized sisters, her body swayed as her feet softly kept time in the dusty earth.

When a belly dancer executes this rhythmic, Basic Lift-Sway Step, she is merely exaggerating the native principle . . . by means of a constant swaying in belly.

This is a step that becomes a good basic for improvisation . . . it can be walked, twisted, and varied.

Assume Basic Position—arms out at shoulder height. Touch floor with right heel and roll up onto ball of foot (just like walking). As foot rolls, lift leg slightly and bring it back to standing position. Belly sways forward with foot.

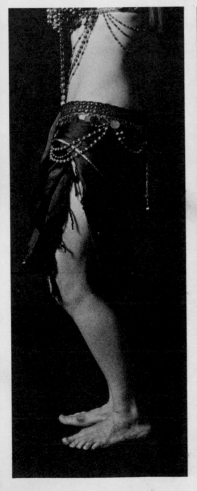  

BREAKING IT DOWN

Assume Basic Position—arms out at shoulder height.

1. Right leg extends forward.

2. Touch floor with right heel and roll up onto ball of foot (just like walking).

3. As foot rolls, lift leg slightly and bring it back to standing position. Belly sways forward with foot.

4. Pelvis sways forward again when right foot is in place.

5. Now, left leg extends forward. Touch floor with left heel and roll up onto ball. As you roll forward and lift to return leg, belly sways.

6. Belly sways again as left foot is in standing position.

UNDERSTANDING IT

If we concentrate on this movement's footwork and leg engineering only, we have this:

1. Right step-roll forward. Lift back.
2. Feet both in place.
3. Left step-roll forward. Lift back.
4. Feet both in place.

If we concentrate on the pendulum sway of the belly, achieved by allowing the belly to move back and forth from the rib cage like a loose swing, we have this:

1. Belly sways as if sliding out to cover front foot.
2. Belly sways just as far forward AND BACKWARD with both feet in place.

MOVING WITH IT

To walk with the Lift-Sway Step, make this simple change:

1. Foot extends forward. Roll from heel up to ball of foot and lift hip.
2. NOW, INSTEAD OF BRINGING FOOT BACK TO STANDING POSITION, make lift but step down on foot to walk forward.
3. Bring left foot in front and repeat. Then continue walking, swaying belly (1) as foot touches forward and (2) as foot steps down.

MAKING IT GREAT

1. Once you have gotten the swing of the basic step, use your arms to accentuate the movements. (Arm movements should originate in the torso and work outward so that they are full, smooth gestures and not flappy, stiff flailings.)
2. Add countermovement with the rib cage or shoulders. PRETEND YOU ARE MOVING UNDER WATER—push and pull against an imaginary weight. RESIST the air around you.
3. Add a twist of the hip . . . as the foot rolls in front of you, bring the round part of the hip around to the front with each leg lift.
4. After you have studied the chapter on finger cymbals, practice this step with them. A good basic rhythm for this step involves three clacks of the cymbals (left-right-left . . . right-left-right . . . left-right-left, etc.) with each of the step's four main movements.

DANCE MASTER PATTERNS
the A, B, C's

PUTTING IT TOGETHER

With just these three basic movements, let's start dancing!

Yes you can—By using the Step Master Chart and the simple Step Pattern Keys.

You have been working on three basic movements:

A. Side-to-Side Sway
B. Figure 8 Sway
C. Basic Lift Step

Add variations for each movement, and you have your first Step Master Chart vocabulary.

A-1	Basic Side-to-Side Sway	Fast or slow
A-2	Basic Side-to-Side Sway	Broad or subtle
A-3	Basic Side-to-Side Sway	Bent knees or on tippy-toes
B-1	Basic Figure 8 Sway	Fast or slow
B-2	Basic Figure 8 Sway	Broad or subtle
B-3	Figure 8 with deeply bent knees	
B-4	Figure 8 Teeter-Totter	
C-1	Basic Step in place	Fast or slow
C-2	Basic Step in place	Broad or subtle
C-3	Basic Step moving forward	

STEP MASTER PATTERNS

Do each step 4 times. Run through each pattern until you no longer "stop and think" about which movement comes next. This gives you practice in making smooth, meaningful transitions from one step to another. Practice these sample patterns, then make up your own.

PATTERN I

A-1	(Basic Side-to-Side)	SLOW (Do 4)
B-1	(Basic Figure 8)	SLOW
C-3	(Basic Lift Step)	FORWARD
A-1	(Return to Side-to-Side)	SLOW

PATTERN II

B-2	(Figure 8)	BROAD
A-1	(Side-to-Side)	FAST
C-1	(Basic Lift Step)	IN PLACE
B-2	(Return to Figure 8)	BROAD

PATTERN III (See what you can do with just one basic.)

A-1	Slow
A-3	Bent knees
A-2	Broadly
A-3	Tiptoes
A-1	Basic slow
A-1	Basic fast

PATTERN IV (This will get you moving around your dance area.)

C-3	Small steps
A-1	Slow
C-3	Large steps . . . in a new direction
B-1	Slow
C-3	Small steps . . . in a new direction

PATTERN V (Moving in up-and-down space.)

C-1	
A-3	Bent knees
B-4	Teeter-Totter
A-3	Tiptoes
C-1	

73

THE HIP LIFTS

the provocateurs

One of the belly dancer's most rhythmically provocative movements. The angular leaning comes from proper use of bent knees. Use it for sultry emphasis of your lower-torso roundnesses, or bounce it around for lively abandon.

BREAKING IT DOWN

1. Assume Basic Position, with knees DEEPLY bent. Extend left foot slightly forward. Incline weight on right leg.

2. Rise up to ball of left foot, keeping heel high off floor. Keep both knees bent . . . but weight on right.

3. Now—for the Hip Lift—straighten left leg, pushing hip and thigh forward (not to side). Keep heel of left foot off ground. Right knee will straighten only slightly.

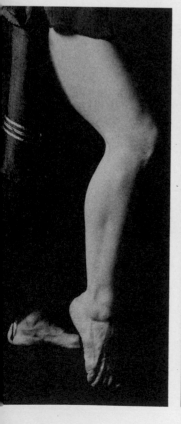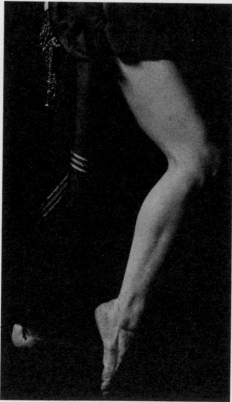

4. Let hip fall back into Basic Position, allowing left knee to bend again.

5. Repeat lift.

Lean back to accentuate the angle of your body. BUT DON'T BEND YOUR BACK . . . as your muscles get conditioned, you will be able to bend that right knee even more.

MAKING IT GREAT

LEANING BACK WITH THE HIP LIFT

1. Lean back to accentuate the angle of your body. BUT DON'T BEND YOUR BACK . . . as your muscles get conditioned, you will be able to bend that RIGHT KNEE even more.

2. Lean your torso backward, TUCK THE PELVIS so that you keep your center of gravity over the right foot . . . and proceed with the Hip Lift.

KEEPING TIME WITH THE HIP LIFT

1. To develop rhythmic use of the Hip Lift, add doubles and triples:
A. In Basic Position for Hip Lift.
B. Execute a Hip Lift forward.
C. Let hip fall back only SLIGHTLY, and push it forward again. Push into floor with ball of left foot to increase control.
D. Practice to music—accentuate the rhythm by combining single, double, and triple Hip Lifts.

MOVING WITH THE HIP LIFT

You can use the Hip Lift to propel yourself in a circle or to the side.

HIP-LIFT CIRCLE

1. Assume Basic Hip-Lift Position.
2. Execute a Hip Lift, let hip fall back again.
3. NOW, AS YOU BEGIN TO EXECUTE A SECOND HIP LIFT, PLACE BALL OF LEFT FOOT SLIGHTLY MORE TOWARD RIGHT. DO YOUR HIP LIFT, LETTING LEFT FOOT PULL YOU TOWARD RIGHT. RIGHT FOOT WILL PIVOT SLIGHTLY.
4. Continue in a circle until you have returned to original position. (A circle in place.)
5. The more you allow hip to fall back with each step, the more you allow left knee to bend on its return to Basic Position, the more of a movement will be executed in the rise and fall of the hip.

MOVING SIDEWAYS WITH HIP LIFT

1. Assume Basic Hip-Lift Position.
2. Execute Hip Lift, to side, not forward.
3. Hold all weight on LEFT FOOT . . . so that right foot is free. Straighten left leg.

4. As Hip Lift is at peak, lift right foot slightly and bring it back down toward left foot.

5. With each Hip Lift, left leg moves slightly to left.

6. KEEP LIFTS AND MOVEMENT OF RIGHT FOOT SMALL. MOVE A FEW STEPS TO LEFT, THEN TRY USING RIGHT HIP AND REVERSE HIP-LIFT PROCEDURE TO RIGHT.

THE ROLLING HIP LIFT

to get things rolling

1. Place index finger on hip.

2. Move hip in circle, using finger to describe the roundness. Work that knee!

3. Remove finger and dance it.

LOWER TORSO CIRCLES
the snake charmers

DANCING IT

WITH RHYTHM

1. Unlike most other belly-dance movements, in which the downbeat (accented beat) is given a forward thrust, the Hip Lift is used to FALL BACK WITH THE DOWNBEAT. If you want to emphasize a beat, execute the Hip Lift so that you fall back into Basic Position as that beat is heard.

WITH EMPHASIS

2. Further emphasis of the back-fall is achieved by giving a slight push with the left foot immediately before falling back with the hip.

WITH VARIATION

3. Vary the amount of space covered by hip . . . vary the number of bounces on each lift . . . vary the speed. Combine a deep, slow Hip Lift with a couple of bouncier doubles.

WITH ARMS

4. Raise right arm, keeping left at shoulder height, to frame your face while you do the Hip Lift.

TRAVELING IN HIPPY CIRCLES

Here comes the ceiling snake . . . the spirals and twists that have mesmerized audiences for some 3,500 years. The smoother the better . . . and again, the legs hold the engineering secrets . . . bending and pushing to allow free-wheeling pelvic and lower torso gliding and whirling.

GETTING READY
an excercise

1. Assume Basic Position.
2. Push left hip out, to left side, holding upper torso as still as possible. *Bounce it out . . . as though you were holding schoolbooks or a toddler on that hip.*

3. Now, push your lower torso as far frontward and center as you can. Keep knees slightly bent. Tuck pelvis under.

4. Now, push right side of hip to right side.

5. Push derriere upward and backward.

6. Return to left-hip position, move on until you can SMOOTH OUT THE HIP POSITIONS AND WIND AROUND IN A LOWER-TORSO CIRCLE. Again . . . attempt to keep upper torso as still as you can.

As you smooth out the circle, bring your feet and legs under smooth

control. Rotate your weight from foot to foot, describing a circle around the outer edge, toes, and heels. This carries your torso around without jerks and halts.

DON'T CHEAT YOUR CIRCLE. . . . Each body will find one or two parts of the "circle" are a little stiff . . . work on that part until the entire circle is smooth and round . . . don't make lop-sided angles anywhere in your belly-dance roundnesses.

Now, push right side of hip to right side.   *Push derriere upward and backward.*

DANCING WITH THE LOWER-TORSO CIRCLE

1. Just as you have executed the preceding demonstration . . . move your lower torso in a smooth circle. MAKE IT BROAD AND SLOW . . . MAKE IT SUBTLE . . . MAKE IT FAST AND INTENSE.

2. Describe circular patterns with a few extra flourishes.

FLOURISH NUMBER ONE *circle within a circle*

UNDERSTANDING IT

Here is the imaginary circle pattern you will describe with your hips and lower torso.

DANCING IT

1. For demonstration purposes, start your big, sweeping, smooth hip and lower-torso circle in the back position. KEEP KNEES WELL BENT AND STAND RELAXED. KEEP RIB CAGE UP—MOVEMENT STARTS AT BOTTOM OF RIB CAGE . . . LEAVE THEM BONES ON THE SHELF.

2. Move torso through left extension, swing around to (A)—directly in front.

3. Now, roll hips around from right to left to describe a smaller circle toward the front of your larger circle.

4. When you have completed one or more smaller circles, return to (A) and continue the circle toward right side and on through backward extension.

5. Repeat . . . vary the movement by making the larger circle slow, the smaller one fast; or the larger circle fast and the smaller one slow.

FLOURISH NUMBER TWO *two circles within a circle*

Here is the imaginary circle pattern you will describe with your lower torso.

1. For demonstration purposes, start your circle in the back position.

2. When left hip arrives at front left (A), describe a small but complete circle over left foot, from left to right and back to (A).

3. Without stopping, move on through forward extension.

4. As right hip arrives at front right (B), describe a small circle over right foot, moving hip from right to left and back to (B).

5. Without stopping, move on through backward extension, and repeat.

Of course, it is best to start your circles at either side. We have indicated starting in back only to make the breakdown more easily understood for practicing.

DANCING WITH HIPPY CIRCLES

1. Here's an intriguing, subtle version: Rise high on the balls of your feet. Execute smooth and quiet circles. Raise arms high over head.

2. Take your circles for a walk. As left hip is extended to left, move left foot forward (a wee step). Continue circle through front extension to right-hip side. As right hip extends to right, move forward with right foot. Continue, alternating.

3. Turn yourself around with a hippy circle. As you execute the Basic Hip Circle, your left leg will give you a push and your right will pivot around. Here's how to do it:

A. As right hip is moving to right side, and weight is on right foot, lift left leg, straighten knee, and set it down just as left hip is moving in from the rear again.

B. Allow right foot to pivot slightly.

C. Work yourself around in this fashion.

(Refer to Hip-Lift Circle)

THE SHIMMIES AND BOUNCES
the enliveners

THE SHIMMY SHAKEDOWN

What makes the belly dancer jingle so? Her belt of coins or beaded fringe quiver so? It's the Shimmy, of course . . . most exciting and colorful quiver ever to come from a dancing body. It looks fantastic and sexy —and it is. It also looks very difficult—which it isn't. Actually, the Shimmy is a movement requiring less muscle ability than most. It's main prerequisite is in learning to relax—to let it all hang out and flap around like a bowlful of jelly being gently jiggled. Many dancers shift into a Shimmy just to give themselves a rest from the more taxing movements. You can use the Shimmy in discothèque rock dancing too—it can be added to any kind of step to inject an electrical quality.

When practicing this, it is very helpful to wear coins around your hips . . . if you haven't gotten around to making your own, tie on a big scarf and attach the noisiest jangles and baubles you have. The jingle will let you know when your Shimmy is at least a reasonable one.

BREAKING IT DOWN

1. Assume the Basic Position. Knees bent. Relax torso; let that belly and derriere hang out. Relax internal (*sphincter*) muscles.

2. Shift weight to right foot, keeping upper body in central position. Do not stiffen shoulders.

3. Let right hip fall to right side as weight is being shifted to right foot. This is the same hip thrust you may have used to tote schoolbooks or a toddler. Left foot rests in place.

4. SMOOTHLY NOW—shift weight to left foot, letting left hip fall to left side to "hold books."

5. THE BASIC SHIMMY IS EXECUTED BY SIMPLY REPEATING THIS WEIGHT CHANGE SMOOTHLY AND WITH INCREASING RAPIDITY.

CLUE: You should feel a pleasant loose vibration—a flopping kind of quiver—in the buttocks and upper inner thighs as you make your Shimmy.

KEEP YOUR KNEES BENT . . . SHOULDERS DOWN . . . ARMS RELAXED TRY TO HOLD RIB CAGE AND UPPER TORSO IN PLACE . . . RELAX.

WALKING WITH THE SHIMMY

This one is a bitch! Keep it for your more advanced practice . . . it is WELL worth the effort.

1. Assume Basic Position.
2. Begin Basic Shimmy.
3. Listening to the music, SHIFT WEIGHT slightly to right foot on downbeat.
4. SHIFT WEIGHT slightly to left foot on next downbeat. DON'T STOP THE SHIMMY! Your rhythm count is:

> RIGHT-two-three-four
>   shift
> LEFT-two-three-four
>   shift
> RIGHT-two-three-four, etc.

This is similar to how you learned the Basic Shimmy. Now you are shifting weight within the Shimmy. You will find that when you are able to put some speed into this movement, it becomes much easier. The impetus of your movement carries you along as much as your muscular efforts.

5. NOW FOR THE WALK. Relax! You're not really going far. To begin, just move a couple of inches with each step . . . even one inch.
6. Continuing the weight-shift Shimmy, your first forward step will come when the weight is on the right foot—at that moment, the left foot will inch forward. On the next downbeat, the weight will shift to the left foot, and the right foot will inch forward. Between steps, the weight will be on both feet as usual.

YOU MIGHT FEEL LIKE A WADDLING DUCK AT FIRST . . . GO RIGHT AHEAD AND WADDLE. ONCE YOU'VE GOTTEN THE KNACK, THEN YOU CAN WORK ON MAKING THE SHIMMY WALK PRETTY.

DANCE MASTER PATTERNS
the D, E, F, and G's

PUTTING IT TOGETHER WITH
THE DANCE MASTER KEY

YOU NOW HAVE THREE ADDITIONAL BASIC MOVEMENTS

D   Hip Lifts
E   Hip and Lower-Torso Circles
F   Shimmies
G   Crossover

AND VARIATIONS FOR EACH MOVEMENT

D-1 Basic Hip Lift, Singles or Doubles
D-2 Hip Lift in a Circle
D-3 Sideways Moving Hip Lift

E-1 Basic Hip/Lower-Torso Circle
E-2 Circle Within a Circle
E-3 Two Circles Within a Circle

F-1 Simple Basic Shimmy
F-2 Walking with Shimmy
F-3 Shimmy Bounce

G-1 Crossover
G-2 Crossover moving
G-3 Crossover with Shimmy

STEP MASTER PATTERNS

As with the A, B, C movement patterns, run through each set until you no longer "step and think" about which movement comes next. Practice these sample patterns, then make up your own.

When you have worked over the D, E, F patterns, move on to incorporate A, B, C patterns. You are now working with six basic movements.

PATTERN VI

D-1   Double Hip Lift   FAST
E-1   Basic Hip Circle   SLOW
F-1   Basic Shimmy   FAST
D-1   Double Hip Lift   SLOW

PATTERN VII

D-2   Hip Lift in Circle   SLOW
E-3   Two Circles in Circle
F-2   Walking with Shimmy
D-2   Hip Lift in Circle
F-1   Basic Shimmy   FAST
D-1   Double Hip Lift   SLOW

THE CROSSOVER STEP *a locomotion movement*

1. Transition step: In Basic Position. Right foot crosses over left. Hold.
2. Left foot steps sideways toward left side . . . touch floor with toes; lift and swing hip as you continue to keep weight on right foot.
3. Bring left foot over right and step on it. Keep weight on left foot as
4. Right leg extends to right side . . . touch floor and push with toes, lift and swing hip.

Right foot crosses over left. Repeat from beginning.

AS YOU PRACTICE THIS CROSSOVER STEP, YOU WILL DISCOVER THAT YOU CAN CHANGE YOUR ANGLE OF MOVEMENT AND COVER A LOT OF GROUND.

TO MAKE IT GREAT

Involve the arms for a good effect: As left leg extends to left side, extend left arm out at hip level and hold right arm up. As you change to extending right leg to right side, left arm goes up and right arm goes out.

Give the hip a gentle bounce as you push with your toes.

Now, let's add some movements from the A, B, C chart. Remember, do each movement about 4 times.

PATTERN IX

A-2   Side-to-Side   SLOW
D-1   Hip Lift, Singles
C-1   Basic Step, in place
A-2   Side-to-Side   SLOW

PATTERN X

This one will get you covering space. Keep walking movements SMALL
—belly dancing rarely takes place on huge dance floors.

C-3
D-3 Sideways Hip Lift
F-2 Walking with Shimmy
G-1 Crossover

Five

PUTTING IT ALL TOGETHER
THE BELLY DANCE
how to make it yours

Here it is, the glorified abdomen, "seat" of all human beginnings, the joyous round mound that is the energy center of the belly dance.

Stimulating as belly undulations may be, their use in dance originated as a magical ritual: The celebration of the life forces realized therein; a physical symbolism that fluttered to the source of mankind itself.

As with such important things as altars and bellies, it is fitting that a proper surrounding be created. In the belly dance, the entire frame works around the abdominal center. The whole body makes the belly a structure for movement.

It may seem strange that the use of the belly alone is only a small part of the dance, reserved for brief improvisational flurries in the faster part of the dance, and given a brief solo of undulations during the Taxim and Tcheftetelli.

Every movement of the rib cage has some effect on the belly; the hip twists gently drag the abdominal muscles along. Just breathing—a dancer does a lot of the deep variety—is reflected by belly response.

But when it is time to let the belly do her solo, everything else takes a back seat, and hearts beat faster all around.

HERE ARE SOME GENERAL INSTRUCTIONS FOR BELLY WORK

1. Let the torso muscles relax to the extreme.
2. Basic Position is essential—bend those knees.
3. Don't work on belly movements right before or after eating.
4. Work both on isolation movements using belly muscles only and on belly movements that allow more of the body to come into play. You get bigger movements if your legs and rib cage are co-operating, even helping your body engineer itself so that the belly movements are given sway and twist to make them even more prominent.
5. Get into yourself . . . no movement instills such internal physical and emotional response as working those belly muscles in deep, rhythmic play. Enjoy yourself.

FRINGE BENEFITS: Nothing, no girdle, no diet, works such wonders on toning the abdominal muscles and firming the skin as these belly movements. Loose flab gets a younger, firmer tone—bellies that just lack personality develop a beautiful feminine curve. This is absolutely not meant for those who prefer waist-cinch-inspired fashions. Only men need flat bellies.

1. THE SIMPLE BELLY-BELLY SHIFT.
    A. Basic Position . . . PUSH PELVIS FORWARD.
    B. In a fashion similar to a small Figure 8, push hip forward as you shift weight in a lilting roll from side to side.
    C. Keep belly relaxed. Shift back and forth without pausing, slowly and smoothly. You will see the belly muscles will swell and roll from side to side.

YOU DO NOT NEED TO CONSCIOUSLY WORK YOUR BELLY MUSCLES.

2. THE RIB-LIFT BELLY SWING.

A. A natural belly movement occurs when you execute a smooth rib lift, such as the 10 O'clock Roll, or even the basic rib cage exercise in the

3. HEAVE-HO—rolling the stomach muscles—IN THE BATHTUB, YET. This one is extremely effective—and, naturally, takes a more conscientious effort. In other words, it needs diligent practice. A GOOD PLACE TO PRACTICE IS IN THE BATHTUB—filled with enough water to totally cover your body. Drop in some fragrant oils and languor awhile to get really relaxed.

A. Lie fairly flat in the tub, your neck and head against the back. Put a washcloth behind you if the porcelain is too cold.

B. Draw the belly muscles (from lower abdomen) upward, toward rib cage.

C. Now, when you have drawn the muscles upward, bear down by pushing the muscles more inward—toward the backbone—and push the muscle back down to the lower abdomen.

D. Work toward developing a smooth, oval-shaped description with the belly muscles. You are pushing out, pulling up, then pulling in and pushing down.

4. THE DIAPHRAGM FLUTTERS—the *danse du ventre*.

A. Stand in Basic Position (or stay stretched out in your tub). Let belly muscles fall, relaxed and hanging out.

B. Start making gasping breaths high in the throat. Minimize the facial response—this is a deep, dark secret, and we don't want anyone to give it away by obviously breathing heavily. After some practice, you may find this movement bringing better results with the throat closed—and the panting only mimicked.

5. DEEP BREATHING—doing what comes naturally.

A. As you breathe from the diaphragm, you can feel a response in the belly. Exaggerate this response WITHOUT co-ordinate breathing. Push the belly out and smoothly suck it back in. Do this in time with music— sometimes deeply and slowly, other times in rapid succession.

6. COMBINATIONS.

Just as with your other movements, work on combining the various belly actions. Start with the Basic Belly Shift, move into a Heave-Ho muscle roll, add a few Flutters, back into the Basic Belly Shift, then on into a Deep Breathing in-and-out set.

DANCING WITH THE BELLY ROLL

Most belly movements are done during the slow, languorous part of the dance. The music itself compels you to move with a sensual intensity. Let your position and facial expressions fit the mode—that hush from your audience, a considerable contrast from the more lively response of your faster dancing, indicates the old belly-roll blues are doing their thing, mesmerizing and hypnotizing them with the rhythmic expression centered in your belly.

ZILLS, DARLING, ZILLS

you and the finger cymbals

You can't do a belly dance without finger cymbals. At first, you might think it's just the opposite . . . it seems almost impossible to do a simple movement while playing the cymbals at the same time. We can't give you any easy out here . . . it's a matter of getting used to doing three or four things at the same time. You've got to put your time in and get acquainted with the cymbals. Without a doubt, you *will* get used to it. Before you know it, playing the cymbals will be as natural as snapping your fingers . . . they go on their own kind of automatic pilot.

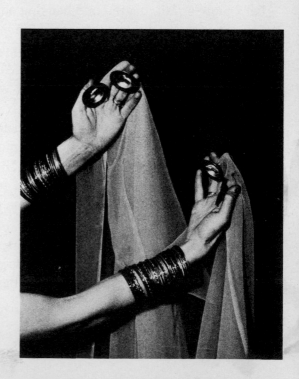

Finger cymbals are generally played as a percussion instrument. Made of various metals, often ornate and domed, the small cymbals are attached to the thumbs and second finger of each hand.

Try your steps with the cymbals on your hands, so you will at least get used to the feeling. Your arms will soon get stronger, and you won't even know you've got as much as a pound of brass riding your fingers.

Where do you get your "zills"? Most large cities have Middle Eastern or general import stores where cymbals are available or can be ordered. All musical instrument stores carry a domestic version of the finger cymbal. Either imported or homemade will do.

Imported cymbals are usually outfitted with narrow, tubular plastic finger loops. You will definitely want to replace these loops with a wider, flat elastic (¼ inch to ⅜ inch wide). The tubular plastic just plain hurts the fingers and does not anchor cymbals properly.

Try on your cymbals . . . follow the rhythm patterns you will soon read . . . try to make the sound pleasant. Experiment . . . play to rock-and-roll records . . . anything to start getting a natural connection.

Cymbals are usually played as an accompanying percussion line, sometimes as a counter rhythm, sometimes directly in time with the drum. (The rhythms are more simple and consistent than those played by the drummer.)

Pretty little things that they are, zills are capable of producing a wide range of sounds, from clear bell-like rings to earthy clacking. Experiment with yours . . . hit them lightly on the edges, clap them together with more force.

Now, down to the essentials of "zilling."

PUTTING ON THE CYMBALS

Place one cymbal on each thumb and second finger (see illustration page 92), with elastic loop on top of hand, cymbal on palm side. The elastic circles the second finger close to the second joint—just above or just below. Adjust the cymbals so that they will lay flat on a table top when you lay your palms down.

WARMING UP: Without striking cymbals, move your hands in large wrist circles to build confidence that your cymbals won't fall off while playing.

PLAYING THE CYMBALS

Most of the movement in playing the cymbals comes by LIGHTLY bringing the thumb cymbal to meet the finger cymbal. If you work each cymbal with the same energy, you will produce a harsher tone. To produce varying tones, vary the angle and pressure.

KEEP THE WHOLE HAND RELAXED!

BELL TONE:

Lightly tap edge of thumb cymbal to edge of finger cymbal.

MUTED TONE:

Bunch thumb and finger so that the cymbals are in contact with more of hand. This reduces the sharper bell tone to a quiet, intriguing, muted tone.

FULL TONE:

Relax wrists extremely. Let thumb cymbal fall easily to finger cymbal. Keep a graceful, lilting movement to playing.

ACCENTED TONES:

Any rhythm is based on a certain number of beats being accented, usually with some regularity. To accent a tone on the zills, just apply slightly more pressure.

PLAYING THE CYMBALS *basic rhythm pattern*

Practice this first without any other body part moving.

Working within a simple four-beat measure, follow this chart. Note accented beats.

BEAT	1	2	3 ′	4
	R	L	R ′	pause
	L	R	L ′	pause
	R	L	R ′	pause
	L	R	L	pause

THE GALLOP RHYTHM

This is the most versatile and most standardly used rhythm pattern. Instead of a simple alternating clack, you will make two clacks with the right hand, only one with the left. It usually lends itself to better faster rhythms than the simple basic rhythm. We call it the Gallop because it suggests just

95

that moving rhythm. Start slow, and work up speed, keeping the rhythm consistent.

1	2	3	4
R	R	L	pause
R	R	L	pause

CYMBAL ROLLS

Requires a bit more agility . . . again, start slow and build speed, working for an even beat.

1	2	3	4
R L R	L	R L R	L

COMBINATIONS

Once you are well acquainted with the basic rhythm possibilities, you can start improvising and using combinations. Here's a common mixed pattern. Repeat several times.

1	2	3	4
R	L	R,	pause
L	R	L,	pause
R	L	R	L
R	L	R,	pause

DANCING WITH YOUR CYMBALS

Take a simple movement, or a Dance Master Pattern, put on the record, and work with the cymbals until you feel comfortable in your new two-fold experience. Keep your arms graceful and your wrists relaxed. It will feel awkward at first . . . but soon you will be executing the same flattering arm postures with the cymbals as without. From this point on, we recommend you consider your dancing and your cymbals inseparable. (Except for your exercises, never practice without them, even if they are just riding along, held in ready silence.)

Finger cymbals are employed by a belly dancer during the faster parts of the dance, and occasionally, if she is very sure of the specific and insistent Tcheftetelli rhythm, as a dramatic response in the low part of the dance. It is not necessary to play the cymbals at all times during the Beledi—but most dancers just let their hands start doing what comes naturally, and those cymbals take over while the dancer dances.

UNVEILING THE SECRETS
dance of the seven veils

When the dance of the seven veils was performed by Salome you can bet the audience was held spellbound, veil after veil after veil, intent on what was going to be revealed next. Veiling is, after all, a matter of unveiling.

No one uses seven veils anymore. Just one well tucked, and equally well untucked, swath of gossamer will do. You won't find any gossamer—rayon chiffon or nylon will do. Rayon clings better—nylon tends to be slippery. When selecting fabric for your veil, try it out for flutter and softness. Stiff nylon will be as flattering as newspaper. Two and a half yards is fine for dancers of average height. A little less if you are shorter, more if you are taller.

Working with your veil can well become the most fun of all your practice sessions. Once you learn how to put it on, practice taking it off and using it in front of a mirror. Pose with it; play with it. Make it wings; make it a demure cover up; make it a swirl; make it an enticing tent. It is probably easier to dance with the veil in your hands than without it—such a prop, such a plaything, such an image enhancer. You can hide behind it for a luscious, private moment. You can wrap it around the head of an enchanted admirer and get some audience involvement. You can toss it off like a wild bird, to float sullenly into a colorful pile at the edge of your dancing area.

But before you can play with your diaphanous wings, you have to take them off. And before you can take it off, you have to put it on.

The dancer makes her entrance with the veil attached, mysteriously tucked into her bra top and skirt. It remains tucked in place throughout the first and faster part of the dance. It adds to all movements, enhancing each bounce and shimmy, accentuating spirals and turns, building a mystique that will reach its peak at the point of unveiling.

PUTTING ON THE VEIL *basic tuck style*

1. Drape the veil over the left shoulder (A) with half the veil falling in front and half in back.
2. Tuck into bra strap on top of shoulder. (B)

3. Pick up top end of front portion and tuck into belt at right hip. (C) Let bottom end drape freely.

4. Pick up top edge of back portion and tuck into girdle at right rear hip. (D)

5. Adjust veil across bra top, making another tuck at right collarbone so that your torso is hidden—veiled. (E)

This is an attractive, workable style in which to attach your veil. Experiment with it—let one side hang, make your tucks a few inches higher or lower; find the veiling style that looks best on you. After a couple sessions with your veil, putting it on will be second nature.

It is good to use one finger when tucking in the veil at your hips . . . one precise, long poke to make sure it is well caught and at the same time, will be un-caught without tugging and twisting.

Tuck into bra strap on top of shoulder. (B) Pick up top end of front portion and tuck into belt at right hip. (C) Let bottom end drape freely.

Once your veil is on, you don't think about it until the Taxim and Tcheftetelli—the slow part of the dance.

TAKING OFF THE VEIL

There have been sensational, dramatic dancers who can get away with ripping the veil off in one dynamic yank . . . but most dancers enjoy the process of dancing the veil off, slowly and so organically that no one is aware they are doing it. In other words, it is now time to practice dancing the veil off . . . not just standing there and making a tug, looking at the tuck and just commonly yanking it off. Each movement of unveiling is intrinsic to the dance itself. Stay relaxed, take your time, don't worry if you drop a corner and have to rescue it. Move your hands and arms gracefully.

Pick up top edge of back portion and tuck into girdle at right rear hip. (D) Adjust veil across bra top, making another tuck at right collarbone so that your torso is hidden— veiled. (E) Insert fingers of right hand just above tuck at right front hip (tuck C). Pull gently forward and outward, releasing veil from girdle.

You will soon grow accustomed to handling the veil with hands that still are bearing finger cymbals. Many astute professionals suggest using only the last two fingers on each hand (those without the cymbals) for all veil work, but this is a skill that requires considerable practice and adeptness.

NOTE: Your finger cymbals are on the thumb and second finger of each hand—keep this in mind as you maneuver the veil.

CLOSE-UP OF HANDS, CYMBALS, AND VEIL: YOU WILL USUALLY FIND IT EASIEST TO WORK THE VEIL WITH THE INDEX FINGER AND THE THIRD FINGER.

REMOVE THE VEIL SLOWLY . . . WITH PRACTICE, YOU WILL LEARN JUST HOW HARD TO TUG AND PULL TO GRACEFULLY UNTUCK THE VEIL FROM YOUR COSTUME.

REMEMBER—WORK TOWARD "DANCING" THE VEIL OFF. DON'T STOP AND LOOK AT WHAT YOUR HANDS ARE DOING . . . KEEP ON DANCING, EVEN IF THE MOVEMENT BECOMES MORE SUBTLE, SIMPLE ENOUGH TO ALLOW THE VEIL TO BE EFFECTIVE.

DANCING OFF THE VEIL *a simple procedure*

A fairly uncomplicated way to get it off—dancing all the while. Use graceful movements and keep the beauty of the veil in mind—this is no ordinary striptease.

1. Insert fingers of right hand just above tuck at right front hip (tuck C). Pull gently forward and outward, releasing veil from girdle.
2. Bring right arm upward, pulling veil across body toward right, extending arm sideways. This movement will release veil at tuck A and tuck B—shoulder strap tucks. Use a firm but gentle pressure to make sure the veil gets untucked.
3. Bring left hand inside veil directly out from left shoulder. Grasp upper edge of veil with thumb and index finger.
4. Let left hand glide along upper edge of veil, around the shoulder, toward the left side. When hand arrives slightly behind left hip, firmly grasp veil and pull backward and outward to release back hip tuck (tuck D).
Your veil is now free to work with.

DANCING IT OFF

a more intricate unveiling

1. Bend right arm at elbow, slip hand inside edge of veil at (E)—right shoulder tuck. Gently release veil from tuck, keeping right hand INSIDE veil as you lift it outward, holding veil with index finger underneath, second finger on top.

Bring right arm upward, pulling veil across body toward right, extending arm sideways. This movement will release veil at tuck A and tuck B—shoulder strap tucks. Use a firm but gentle pressure to make sure the veil gets untucked. Bring left hand inside veil directly out from left shoulder. Grasp upper edge of veil with index and middle finger.

Let left hand glide along upper edge of veil, around the shoulder, toward the left side. When hand arrives slightly behind left hip, firmly grasp veil and pull backward and outward to release back hip tuck (tuck D).

Your veil is now free to work with.

2. Slide finger down halfway to right hip tuck. Pull forward until veil is taut. Gently increase pull, lifting hand straight out and drawing hip back until tuck C (right hip front) is released.

3. Now, front end of veil is free. Hold right arm behind veil.

4. Bring left arm up inside veil by bending elbow. Grasp veil with left hand, pulling tuck B (left shoulder) free. Your veil is now held in front of you, about a foot out from body.

5. Veil is flowing around behind body, ending in back tuck.

Bend right arm at elbow, slip hand inside edge of veil at (E)—right shoulder tuck. Gently release veil from tuck, keeping right hand INSIDE veil as you lift it outward, holding veil with index finger underneath, second finger on top. Slide finger down halfway to right hip tuck. Pull forward until veil is taut. Gently increase pull, lifting hand straight out and drawing hip back until tuck C (right hip front) is released.

Bring left arm up inside veil by bending elbow. Grasp veil with left hand, pulling tuck B (left shoulder) free. Your veil is now held in front of you, about a foot out from body.

Veil is flowing around behind body, ending in back tuck.

NOW YOU ARE UNVEILED

YOU AND THE VEIL CAN NOW DANCE TOGETHER . . . LET THE VEIL WAFT THROUGH THE AIR. It has a personality of its own, and by paying attention to its billows, drapings, and flights, you can work with it to produce flowing beauty and ever-changing forms. Sometimes the veil will frame your movements, sometimes the both of you will be lost in a whirl of color.

Experiment in front of a mirror with these examples, and work out some of your own.

DISPOSING OF THE VEIL IN FRIENDLY FASHION

As the Taxim continues, you will want to discard the veil to allow you to continue with your slow movements unencumbered. Disposing of the veil should be part of your dance . . . not a perfunctory chucking it away. Here are some effective ways of doing it:

1. Fling it into a far corner of the dance area.
2. Find a willing man . . . drape the veil over his head and yours. Then wrap it around his head and shoulders . . . he'll gladly return it to you when your dance is finished.
3. Gracefully drape the veil around your own hips, making a single knot on your hip. This can be done gracefully if you make each lift and tuck smooth and poised.
4. Gather the veil in one hand until it is bunched into a small frothy shape. Set it down as you make a turn.

MAKE AN OVERHEAD CANOPY.

THE SPHINX LOOKS OUT.

THE FRAME.

BODY DRAPE.

SWIRLING CAPE.

THE BIG FRAME-UP
using arms and hands

The next question is . . . what do we do with our arms? No matter how well you learn to move your rib cage, belly, hips, and legs, no dance is worth a second glance unless there is a balance, a frame, a line of expression. These two upper appendages, which we allow to atrophy in our daily life, become the wings of improvisation when we dance. The problem is that in our daily atrophies, we rarely allow the arms to move even a small percentage of their potential. We raise our arms overhead only to get a hat or can of turtle soup off the top shelf; we rarely move our arms backward, to say nothing of outward. Most arms are in rather shaky condition when they are first forced into dancerly positions . . . but with constant awareness and a little effort, the arms are soon flying.

There is no need to master a standard pattern for your arm movements—we would hope rather that your arms become your own personal addition to your dancing. As your legs and feet are the rhythmic workhorses in the belly dance, so are your arms the free-form improvisers.

Work with your mirror to discover the arm positions that look best on you. Arms are very individual. Sharp pointed elbows need to be considered —so do flabby upper arms. Find ways to hold your arms so that the most flattering angles are presented to your "audience."

The arms literally add composition and line to your entire body. Experiment with that mirror image—consider the total effect.

Arms serve to frame your face. Explore the possibilities. Experiment with symmetrical poses, with asymmetrical lines, with sweeps and circles and reaches and pulls.

Arm movement should originate in the torso. Start the motion in your "heart" . . . use the back muscles. Let the energy flow outward. Otherwise you look as though you're drowning.

Roundness and balanced line is what you're after. Images help: Pretend you are wrapping the arms around the trunk of an invisible and huge tree; reach out for a loved one; offer some invisible fruits in the palms of your hands; pick flowers off a high-trailing vine.

Remember, you will be holding your cymbals in your hands . . . and, during part of the dance, edges of your veil. It is vital that your use of arms becomes second nature to you. Here are some pointers . . . and errors to avoid.

IN THE BEGINNING

Hold arms well out from body, to sides, a little below shoulder height. THINK ROUND. Keep shoulders natural and relaxed, no hunching. Practice all your movements with your arms held thusly . . . it will develop staying power. And, oh, how it might tire you at first, particularly in the upper arm.

As you begin to move your arms as part of the body dancing, go slow at first. Do not make sharp, sudden transitions. Check out your mirror.

If you must move all the time, let your arms remain fixed and move your hands with a loose wrist. This is extremely feminine.

Don't be afraid of keeping your arms in one or two comfortable, flattering positions. A little movement is considerably more attractive than too much.

THE FLAILING CHA-CHA-CHA GIRLS

Here are a few common mistakes that you should try to avoid:

1. Flailing the arms as if you were paddling a boat.
2. Clenching the fist.
3. Stiffening or hunching the shoulders.

4. Doing the rat-a-tat-tat-cha-cha—describing tight little circles in front of your bosom.

5. Using your hands to (unconsciously?) cover yourself up. Keep arms away from the torso. Do not cross hands in front of you. Do not assume prayerlike attitudes.

6. Moving the arms too much. Constant motion is like no motion at all . . . there's no contrast or control. At first, it is far better to just hold your arms, slightly rounded, a little lower than shoulder height—and WELL OUT FROM YOUR BODY. If you must move something all the time, work on your wrists and hands . . . it can only look extremely feminine.

HERE ARE SOME ARM POSITIONS THAT WORK WELL FOR THE BASIC BELLY DANCE.

1. Basic Position. (Arms out at sides, rounded.)
2. Overhead Position. (Don't let the chin fall out.) Keep arms *high* overhead for beautiful effects. Drooping hands cause elbows to protrude.
3. Forward Position, angle. (Great for countermovements emanating in the back . . . that push-and-pull restraint that adds intensity.)

Forward position, angle. (Great for countermovements emanating in the back . . . that push-and-pull restraint that adds intensity.)

4. Up-and-Out (low). (One arm above head, the other extending forward from mid-torso.)

5. Up-and-Out (high). (Great for round alternations.)

6. Close-in—for hip movements.

7. Elbow bent behind head; other arm pushing out.

Up-and-out (low). (One arm above head, the other extending forward from mid-torso.)
Up-and-out (high). (Great for round alternations.)

Close-in—for hip movements.

Elbow bent behind head; other arm pushing out.

CHANGING POSITIONS WITH THE ARMS

Naturally, you're not going to freeze your arms into one position for your entire dance, no matter how flattering it is. To do so would be to defy expression completely.

To use the arms effectively, they should complement your body, without distracting. Arm movements will lend themselves to the body movements. You will find the arm positions will often spring naturally from what the rest of you is doing. But it's not all that easy. You must practice to develop technical skill, control, and grace.

When you are dancing, let your arms go to the positions that seem easiest and best—with repeated checks in the mirror.

Transitions with arm movements are even more vital than with hip or leg movements. PRACTICE ARM MOVEMENTS ALONE FOR AWHILE, MAKING TRANSITIONS FROM ONE POSITION TO ANOTHER. In making a transition, let the arms follow a controlled but relaxed pathway into the new position. Each little inch of that pathway becomes a position in itself. Think of your hands as birds in flight bound to earth by the leash of your arms.

SPINS AND TURNS
around you go

A dance without some spinning, turning, round pivoting, and whirling is one-dimensional. Slow turns enable you to contact your entire audience; to encounter all directions of space around you; to present your image (costume, form, and you) in a three-dimensional sweep. Faster spins express excitement and abandon. And when you can't think of anything else to do at a given moment, there's nothing like a whirl or two to get your juices reactivated.

A SLOW TURN

1. From standing position, cross left foot over right, landing 12 inches away.

2. Lift onto balls of both feet and turn yourself around. You are now facing the opposite direction.

3. Repeat: cross left foot over right, lift onto balls, and pivot yourself back to original direction.

NOTE: Absorb the lift in your legs; work for a smooth turn with no head bobbing.

A SPIN—FASTER AND WITH SPOTTING

1. Repeat slow-turn procedure several times.

2. Now is when your old ballet lessons may prove valuable. Remember spotting? You can work without it for a couple of spins, but any real whirling will leave you dizzy without this classical dancing technique.

SPOTTING IS SOMETHING TO PRACTICE

1. As you prepare to turn from your original position, focus your eyes on an object straight ahead. As your body starts turning, keep your head focused thereon as long as you can.

2. Your body is now facing the opposite direction. Your head snaps around to quickly refocus on the spotting object, and your body follows.

122

THE PERSIAN PIVOT

This is a graceful stepping turn, fast or slow, and when incorporated with suggested use of arms, a real ethnic charmer.

THE ARMS:

1. Hold right arm with elbow bent, let head look out over shoulder and upper arm to right and back.
2. Let left arm curl behind left hip, with elbow slightly rounded.

NOW FOR THE TURN:

1. Hold weight on flat right foot. Raise onto ball of left foot.
2. With tiny steps, push yourself around with left foot. At each push, right heel slightly lifts so it can help you pivot around.

NOTE: Don't attempt more of a spin than you are comfortable with . . . no matter how breathtaking your whirl, it does little for your dance if you stumble and fall in your dizziness.

PRACTICE SPINS AND TURNS WITH YOUR VEIL . . . FLY A KITE, MOVE YOUR WINGS, WHIRL A FRENZY OF COLOR WITH YOUR CAPE.

FLOOR WORK
just like a snake

"She walks . . . She talks . . . She crawls on her belly like a reptile . . ."
. . . some old carny barker advertising Little Egypt . . .

When it comes right down to it, there's nothing like a good roll on the floor to convey the serpentine spirit released in belly dancing.

The perspiration from the fast introduction of her dance set gleams on her skin as the drums still and the oud player wails his sonorous, sensual improvisation. With seeming ease, the dancer has dropped to her knees, her hair trailing to the floor behind her as she lowers her body in a graceful arch. Writhing gracefully, she turns and extends a jeweled foot, her raised hip spiraling in serpentine twist. She suddenly twists about, coiling and churning in a blur of color and coins. Her hands gather her mass of black hair as she rises back to her knees, sweeping up from the waist in a final climax of lithe ecstasy. The snake is ready to strike.

Can you imagine a belly dance without all that? It's not as hard as it sounds, but it certainly is as dramatic an image as any dance form has ever called forth.

The ecstasy is up to you. Here are some basic instructions.

GETTING DOWN TO IT . . . GRACEFULLY

How to lower yourself to the floor:

1. From standing position, do a Figure 8 as you gradually bend knees. Continue with Figure 8 until in deep knee-bend position.

2. To get completely down from that position, execute a gentle shoulder Shimmy as a point of distraction while you gently lower knees to floor.

NOW THAT YOU'RE ON YOUR KNEES . . .

You will find that you can now execute several steps you learned standing up . . . the Side-to-Side, Figure 8, shoulder and hip Shimmies, Rib-Cage Lifts, Hip Circles . . .

You also can vary these movements by the various positionings:

1. Ride a U-shaped path from sitting up at one side, letting the derriere sweep in a backward half circle, and sitting up again at the other side.

2. Using the side-to-side movement, slowly undulate down from an upright kneeling position to a position just above the feet, with the derriere almost touching the heels—but instead of resting there, continue Side-to-Side movement smoothly back into upright sitting position.

THE "BACK BENDS"

the every-woman acrobatics

A WORD OF CAUTION—Whereas these are not true back bends in the acrobatic sense, there may be certain bodies that should not attempt these movements. It is not necessary to do a back bend . . . just good movements in the kneeling position will suffice.

These back bends do not require you to use your back to support yourself. Again, it's a matter of engineering your body so that your weight is supported by the legs and arms.

THE YOGA BEND

1. Still on your knees, grasp heels or ankles with hands.

Still on your knees, grasp heels or ankles with hands.

Arms will bend as you lower shoulders toward heels. CONTINUE LOWERING ONLY AS FAR AS YOU FEEL FIRMLY SUPPORTED.

In upright kneeling position: arms extended outward at shoulder level.

2. Let head fall backward. Arch back slightly by lifting rib cage.

3. Arms will bend as you lower shoulders toward heels. CONTINUE LOWER-ING ONLY AS FAR AS YOU FEEL FIRMLY SUPPORTED.

4. To raise yourself back into kneeling position, straighten arms to push torso back upright.

5. KEEP THAT ARCH THROUGHOUT ENTIRE MOVEMENT. DO NOT COLLAPSE ON THE WAY BACK UP. LET HEAD BE THE LAST PART OF YOUR BODY TO ARRIVE IN THE UPRIGHT FLOOR POSITION.

THE BACK DROP . . . this one requires developed thigh muscles.

There are two basic kinds of back bends; one is arched, the other is straight. This is a straight one . . . a cantilevered bend relying on the knees as the lever. Your thighs and back are in straight alignment, and will remain so throughout the movement. Again . . . your back is not supporting you.

WARM-UP EXERCISE (You may do this for several weeks before your body feels comfortable enough to touch the floor.)

1. In upright kneeling position: arms extended outward at shoulder level.

2. Keeping body in straight line, bend backward from knees and return to upright position.

Keeping body in straight line, bend backward from knees and return to upright position.

3. Go back as far as you can and still return upright. Push from pelvis.

DOING THE BACK DROP

1. Assume upright kneeling position. Spread knees comfortably far apart, forming a solid base. Positioning of the feet depends on comfort.

2. Execute the Back Drop, using the same principle as in the warm-up exercise. GO BACK ONLY AS FAR AS YOU CAN AND STILL RETURN YOURSELF WITH REASONABLE EASE TO UPRIGHT KNEEL. The head, again, is the last part to return upright. It is the lingering lilt of that reluctant head that adds the note of sensual surrender to this or any movement.

DANCING IT UP

As you lower your torso, execute a slow, graceful shoulder Shimmy.

HEADLINE: You can prevent that scrunched up neck by letting your head turn to one side as you go backward.

Go back as far as you can and still return upright. Push from pelvis.

Execute the back drop, using the same principle as in the warm-up exercise. GO BACK ONLY AS FAR AS YOU CAN AND STILL RETURN YOURSELF WITH REASONABLE EASE TO UPRIGHT KNEEL. The head, again, is the last part to return upright. It is the lingering lilt of that reluctant head that adds the note of sensual surrender to this or any movement.

THE CLEOPATRA

Hollywood loved this one . . . every harem vamp ever captured in celluloid was depicted lying on her side, her hip seductively accentuated, holding her head in her hand. Don't let the old stereotype set you off . . . when done well, this is an authentic winner!

GETTING INTO POSITION

1. From upright kneel: sit down to one side, using hand as brace.
2. Extend top leg forward, reclining back on bent elbow. Keep bottom leg bent under.

THE CLEOPATRA LEG ROLL

1. With loose top leg, describe large, full circle with top hip, using bottom hip as anchor.

THE CLEOPATRA FIGURE 8 LEG ROLL

In same position, let foot of top leg "draw" an imaginary Figure 8, from top to bottom. Hip will also be describing a Figure 8, moving in a direction from head to toe, not sideways.

THE CLEOPATRA BRIDGE

1. In same position (lying on side), straighten supporting arm, stiffen top leg and body to raise yourself into a bridge.
2. Move your hips around in swivels and circles. Or . . . if you feel brave . . . try a hip Shimmy.

GETTING BACK ON YOUR FEET

1. Bring knees back under you.
2. Execute Figure 8s as you slowly raise yourself by straightening legs.

PUTTING IT ALL TOGETHER

the makings of dance

An exercise is not dance. A dance step is not dance. A costume is not dance. Music is not dance. For all these elements to be synthesized within your mind and body and come out Dance requires that you put together all your new physical know-how, match it with increasing self-expression, connect with the beat and wail of the music, and offer yourself up to another dimension . . . one in which you cannot intellectualize, practice, apologize, or show-off.

The best way to start dancing is to start spending a few sessions trying to "let go" to the music, to stop counting, to stop coaching yourself "left, right, left, 1-2-3-4, etc."

Belly dancing is improvisational, but it is free only within certain standardized forms. Once you have assimilated the essence of the form, once the ideas and images have become yours, you will improvise with the same ease with which you danced about as a child.

THE FORM OF THE DANCE

a guide from entrance to climax

The belly dancer makes her entrance at the beginning of the Beledi section of an approximately 10–15 minute long set. She usually enters from off-stage, briskly slithering, her cymbals ringing, into the center of the dance area. Her first movement, an audience-encompassing spin or two, establishes contact and stirs up interest in her emerging performance.

During the Beledi, all basic movements may be executed. Don't run from one to another . . . start with one movement, say a Basic Lift Step, and work with it a few measures, then switch to another basic, such as the Crossover Step or Figure 8, and "get into it." Play around with that one for a while, go back to the first, and add another. The Dance Master Patterns are all applicable here.

The general tone of the initial Beledi is one of excitement and vitality, yet because the high drama of the dance is yet to come, there is an air of anticipated mystery and pleasure. The first Beledi is foreplay.

The Beledi comes to an end (you will soon be able to anticipate the end of the song). End the Beledi as you started it—with a spin, culminating in a FREEZE as the music fades into the:

Taxim section, in which the musicians play an improvisational solo. At this time, your cymbals are still; you may begin slowly, seductively yet modestly, removing your veil, keeping your movements slow and sensuous. Sometimes the Taxim is brief, a mere prelude, and you will not have completed your veil removal. Don't rush . . . the veil work can well be extended into the next part of the dance, slow but more rhythmic than the Taxim.

The Tcheftetelli rhythm practically dictates movements to you. Use your basic movements and your favorite Dance Master Patterns, but slow them down. Here's where Belly Rolls are most effective. Add a Shiver or a Shimmy once in a while for electric excitement, but basically, keep it deep and supple. Resist the music . . . pull, hold back. Let all your emotions come into play. Be sultry, be seductive, be haughty, be poignantly dramatic. This is your time to be "a heavy."

This slower part of the dance set is also where you will execute your floor work, snake routines, and back bends. Don't rush into them . . . take your time. (The veil is normally discarded before floor work begins.)

The Tcheftetelli speeds up and you are back in the Beledi rhythm for your finale. Use all your basic movements, lively and abandoned Shimmies, toss your head around, move closer to members of your audience and let your sense of humor show. One of the beauties of belly dancing is, like the music it visualizes, the wide range of emotions expressed—from high sensual drama to playful fun. Be a whole person when you dance.

For your ultimate finale and exit, work your Shimmies in an improvisational ecstasy of your own, and add all the flourish you can before you make your final spin and culminating bow. You are going to be out of breath, your heart will be pounding, your face wet with perspiration. But how alive you will feel! After you catch your breath, just let that natural high take over. You earned it.

(In some cases, a dancer will go on to another Taxim, or, more likely, a Drum Solo in which she and the drummer perform a duet. The sounds of the drum, now let loose for more abandoned improvisation, blending and countering with the cymbals and the coins of the dancer's costume make an exhilarating, intricate encore.)

THE RHYTHMS AND YOU

Middle Eastern music is based on definite rhythm patterns. You are the living, visual expression of these rhythms and rhythmically anchored melodies. The more you listen to Middle Eastern music, the more you will intrinsically understand the beats and patterns. The more you understand them, the more accurate and reflective your dancing will be. The drum, of course, is the pulse and origin of the rhythms. Here then is a brief look at two standard Arabic dance rhythms used in the belly dance.

BELEDI

The Beledi is a four-count rhythm. The deeper sounds of the drum are called "dum," the higher-pitched, more metallic tones are called "tek." The basic Beledi is drummed like this. (Drummers always add their own flourishes and rolls, but listen for this underlying pulse.)

1	2	3	4		
Dum	Dum	Tek	Tek		
	1	2		3	4
	Dum	Tek-tek		Tek	Tek-tek

The final tek-tek is a bridge that connects the entire phrase with the succeeding phrase. The rhythm is merely a repetition of this pattern over and over again.

TCHEFTETELLI

The Tcheftetelli's basic rhythm is usually played slowly, but can be played as fast and lively as is the musicians' style or choice. It also is a four-count rhythm, with two measures.

1-and	2-and	3-and	4-and
Dum	Tek-tek	· Tek-	Tek ·
1-and	2-and	3-and	4-and
Dum	Dum	Tek	(Tek-tek)

Other rhythms you will encounter include the Basic Four; the Turkish Tcheftetelli (similar to the basic Tcheftetelli); and various rhythms counted and named according to the number of beats in a measure. Listen to the record and try to tap out the basic beats you hear. Try working a simple movement so that it begins and ends in time with a measure. Use the accent notes to freeze into position for one beat.

PHRASING

Sing a simple song . . . each natural line of the song is a phrase. A phrase is a musical exhalation. It ends at the natural "breathing space." Your dancing will be more meaningful if you start listening for the phrases in Middle

133

Eastern music and incorporate phrasing into your selection and timing of steps. A simple way to start incorporating phrasing is to execute a movement for the length of one phrase, then switch to another when the next phrase begins. Later you will be able to work more intricately within the phrase. If nothing else, use the phrases to denote the change of direction or choice of movement. In many songs, the phrasing is so explicit that it is only natural to dance accordingly. Other Middle Eastern music, still esoteric to the Western ear, is almost beyond deciphering. In that case, just dance. You might have a better automatic pilot than you imagined.

PATTERNS AND DESIGN

The Dance Master Patterns, and the ones you arrange and collect for yourself, are valuable aides in helping you dance within a pleasing form or design. Don't make totally random jumps from one step to another . . . a smooth transition is part of the dance. And don't feel you must run through your entire repertory, one step after another. Use pattern combinations, return to a basic step, embellish it, change into another step, then go back to the basic before you jump into a new pattern. Don't be afraid to use too few steps. Some of the best professionals use only two or three movements, adding flourishes, improvisational switches and variations of tension, speed, emphasis, and direction. The basic step alone gives you dozens of possibilities. Change your direction and the size of your step; change your arms; change the tension and dynamics. You could go on, phrase after phrase and not be bored or boring! Above all, don't stop and think which step is going to come next. Just keep on practicing until you own your movements. Then connect with the music and let it virtually cast a spell over your body.

HALF-TIME, TIME, AND DOUBLE-TIME

Variations of speed are vital to a dance. In Middle Eastern music, the drum is constantly pulsing out one basic rhythm. Over and within it, the melody varies, always anchored to the beat. Within the combined rhythm patterns, you have several choices of dancing speed.

TIME: The predominant count of the beat; a 1-2-3-4 that is pronounced and easy to follow.

HALF-TIME: Twice as fast as the pronounced beat. Squeezing a 1-2-3-4-5-6-7-8 into the 1-2-3-4. Double fast movements.

DOUBLE-TIME: Twice as slow as the pronounced beat. Stretching a 1-2-3-4 into a 1-2-3-4-5-6-7-8. Half as slow movements.

FREEZE

Remember the old statue-rendering game of Freeze? Try it in your dancing for rhythmically dramatic emphasis. Perhaps the hardest thing to do when you first start to dance is to do nothing at all for a moment or two. But it is so effective . . . it is contrast, balance, suspension, and sculpture.

Within a reasonable connection to the song or rhythm, try freezing into a Hip Lift, or a Side Sway . . . and holding it there for just a second.

Especially within the Taxim, these frozen moments need a certain poise to carry them off. You may feel at first that you are "doing nothing" when you freeze—but with all elements working with you (your eyes, your facial expression, your arms framing you, the music just right) it's a winning image and, as a fringe benefit, a secret moment of rest for you.

THE REAL YOU—EXPRESSION AND DYNAMICS, THE FACE AND HEAD

During most of your practice sessions, you have been working your appendages, your torso, and all the intricacies in between. Your head has been working too—looking down at your feet, counting out a pattern, frowning in the mirror at the more awkward images you conjure at first. But when it comes time to dance, your head has got to move and dance too, so that the total body is expressing.

FIRST AND FOREMOST: Stop looking at your feet . . . or your knees . . . or your belly button. Hold your head up. Let it be as subject to grace and vibrancy as your hands.

TOSS IT AROUND when you want to feel and look more lively; angle it off to the side (a la the Garbo-Twist exercise) when you want dramatic splendor; let it fall back to express submission, to your man or your own musical thrall. Work on your neck exercises until you can.

SLIDE THE HEAD AROUND, using controlled, smooth movements. Let your head slide into the cradle of an uplifted arm; let your body freeze and give them the old abracadabra Snake-Charmer routine.

BE DEMURE . . . BE HAUGHTY . . . BE INVITING . . . with your head, both inside and outside. Head movements intensify a feeling working from the outside (the image) to the inside (the feeling)—and vice versa. What you feel can be transmitted more completely with the proper twist of the head.

As for those vital elements that go along with the head . . . the eyes, mouth, and the hundreds of little muscles that control the facial expression . . . relaxation is the primer, the lubricant, the white canvas on which you will paint the myriad smiles, pouts, flutters, and agonies that add the dimension of artistry and communication to your dance. You don't have to look at your audience all the time . . . yes, there is much room for private moments with lowered eyelids. You don't have to smile all the time . . . to do so would be to wear a frozen mask. But don't get so dramatic you forget to toss in a friendly, audience-warming smile; nor so private you deny eye contact. Among the East Indians, where many belly-dance movements originated, a dancer devotes a great deal of study to mastering eye movements to register the various emotions and moods. Again, practice before your mirror. But when you're dancing, don't use your eyes to watch yourself . . . use them to dance.

COINS AND GOSSAMER
dressing the part

COSTUMES, *a definite unabashed put-on*

The legendary ornaments that adorn a dancer's body provide the physical setting for her external mystique. Take, for instance, the outrageous aura of the Las Vegas show girls; tremendous applause greets these ladies on their meanderings up and down the runway—and all they are doing is just plain walking!

This is great news for you, the beginning dancer. A really together costume can transform a practice session into the real thing—not only with visual appeal, but also with the intensified feelings you experience inside from

137

the pleasant weight of your costume on your body, the way in which the jingling of the coins and baubles inspires you into shimmies, movements, and poses you never dreamed you could attain.

Beautiful costumes are often remarkably simple to construct. The fabrics, well chosen and sewn as little as possible to insure a beautiful, free-flowing shape, can be as inexpensive as $.79 a yard. Your most difficult task in assembling your costume will probably be the all-important bra and girdle, coined or beaded . . . but these take more patience than skill.

You might want to start with a simpler costume for practicing—one made from an old bathing suit, some zingy fringe, and some old necklaces and trinkets.

We have given instructions here for the construction of a coin bra and coin girdle, a fringe bra and fringe girdle, two versions of the skirt, an ethnic dance dress, harem pants, and a marvelously versatile cover-up. You might find that within your own wardrobe are items that might work just as well and will express your own individuality. The costumes herein are a synthesis of authentic ethnic dancer's wear and the more showy cabaret gear that has become virtually standardized now.

There's no need to invest a lot of money into making your costume—just use lots of imagination and love.

THE COSTUME BRA*

1. Purchase a good uplift bra. Look for:
   - Wide-set arm straps.
   - Narrow back strap.
   - Good cleavage, nice front lines.
   - Adequate underlining, if you're spare.
   - Black is a good color. If a bit of the bra itself shows through from under the decorations, it is preferable to white or red. Flesh is great too, but harder to get.
2. Cut out webbing from under arms.
3. Remove padding, if possible.
4. Cover cups of bra with chosen fabric . . . a shiny metallic works well, or an old gold. You can also tint the bra an old-gold tone.
5. Attach edging, gold braid, or trim along arm and back straps.
6. Using already perforated stamp-out coins—available in most notions departments, dime stores, or at bead-supply houses—attach with dental floss, leaving large loop so coin can swing freely. Tie each coin separately.

* See Illustrations.

Attach coins along top of cups, along back strap, and along midriff. (Remember, leave about ¼-inch leeway with your dental floss. By the way, nothing is as strong as that dental floss. Take a word from the experienced . . . plain thread, even buttonhole thread, wears down after a while, letting your coins fly loose.)

7. To finish your bra, attach beading, slender chains, or silk fringe along front of cups. Sew finishing edging to top and bottom of cups.

139

FOR A FRINGE BRA

Use a colored bathing suit top, or dye an old bra. Cover with matching fringe (the 2-inch variety is best). Add an old necklace or two.

THE COSTUME GIRDLE*

1. You will need:
   · Gold-colored satin—the cheap, heavy kind.
   · Old sheeting.
   · Stiffening.
   · Stamp-out coins, sequins, beads, chains.
2. Make a pattern. Using any workable paper, follow the suggested shape (fuller in front and in back, narrow at hips) and make a pattern that fits you. Leave slack for seams and closing.
3. From pattern, cut two pieces of the satin; eight of the old sheeting, one of stiffening.
4. To prepare center section, place four pieces of sheeting on each side of stiffening. Sew together around edges. Then, zigzag entire section for added body, as in quilting.
5. Attach satin piece at edges for outside of girdle.
6. Now, using your individuality and imagination, attach coins, sequins, beads, etc., as in costume bra with dental floss. Coins do not need to be sewed immediately next to each other—let them overlap.
7. Attach edging along upper seam of girdle.
8. Affix sturdy hook and eyes—preferably the kind used in men's pants. The closing is best in front.
9. Attach second satin piece, if desired, as back lining to give girdle a finished look. It will be necessary to attach the lining piece by hand.

FOR A FRINGE GIRDLE

Attach two or three rows of fringe to a sash or scarf—wrap around your skirt. For practice, attach fringe to a bikini bottom and wear over leotards.

COVERING UP THE TRICKERY

Skirts and harem pants are worn at the hipline, fitting snugly beneath your costume girdle. In belly dancing, no matter what your costume, your beautiful legs are always demurely covered, except for the quick flashes through the slits of your skirt. Since belly-dance movements are all engineered (without a skirt, you may think the movements look grotesque) the

140

cover-up serves to keep your hard-working legs hidden away, and your undulating torso appears to be floating gracefully above a swath of chiffon.

SKIRTS . . . to cover up your trickery

STRAIGHT-GATHERED SKIRT WITH SPLITS*

1. Purchase about 6 yards of chiffon-type fabric. The inexpensive varieties work just as well.

2. Cut into two sections; one, 1½ yards, the other, 4½ yards.

3. Hem all edges except selvages.

4. Sew 1-inch runner on top selvage of fabric. This will be used for the ½-inch elastic runner waistband.

5. Affix safety pin to end of elastic . . . thread through runner, leaving sufficient length to work with. Pin band to fit hips.

6. Sew ends of elastic together. The smaller panel forms the front of skirt; the slits match up with the front of your legs; the larger panel sweeps around from the front to cover the back.

7. Try on skirt. Measure hem . . . should fall just at ankles so you don't trip over the skirt . . . remember, you dance with knees slightly bent.

NOTE: Weights or trim may be sewn around the bottom hem to give the skirt more body and flair in turns and swirls.

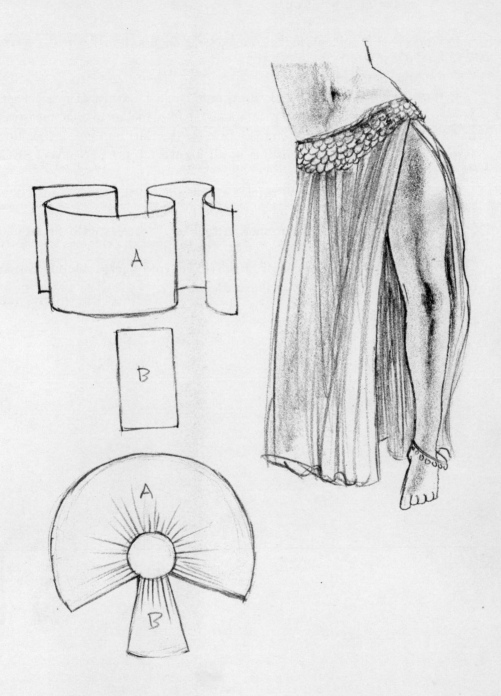

DRAPED SKIRT*

the Egyptian look

1. Works best in soft fabric that drapes well, such as jersey, crepe, certain rayons. You will need about 4 yards.

2. Fold fabric in half.   .

3. With pencil or tailor's chalk, draw semicircle for waist at one corner. Measure on your body from hip to ankles. Add 3 inches to that measurement. Now, trace a semicricle on the fabric for the skirt bottom . . . making sure it is equidistant from waistline at all points. CUT INTO TWO SECTIONS.

4. Sew hem at bottom. Sew runner at top for elastic band. Finish side seams.

5. Run elastic through top runner. Attach ends of elastic to fit around your hips.

6. Put on skirt. Tuck one corner of skirt front into back, tuck one corner of skirt back into front hip. (See illustration.)

HAREM PANTS *

for dancing or wearing

1. Requires about 3 yards of fabric. A sheer works well . . . try a less transparent Paisley or soft print for an earthy effect or for wear-arounds.

2. Divide fabric in half, making two 1½-yard pieces.

3. Sew according to illustration; measure crotch, from center seam to hips. Add 2 inches for elastic drawstring runner, one inch for the waist and the second at each leg bottom. Sew each leg into tube UP TO CROTCH. Then connect crotches of each piece, joining the two tubular legs together.

4. Sew 1½-inch runner at each leg bottom.

5. Draw elastic through at waist and leg bottoms. Elastic at leg should fit comfortably AROUND MID-CALF.

6. Put on harem pants. Pull leg bottom up inside so that elastic fits over calf, allowing fabric to billow at ankles.

(Refer to illustration.)

THE BELEDI DRESS

Great for the more modest dancer. A cover-up that lacks nothing in appeal, authenticity, or movability. For those of you who are hesitant to let it all hang out—stretch marks and folds and wrinkles and all—this is the answer, and has been for hundreds of years. Even at this time in Egypt, the Beledi dress is worn by performers who by decree of law must not show bare midriffs.

The Beledi dress is a sheer swath of fabric falling from shoulders to ankles, caught at the hips by your costume belt or a fringed scarf. Sparkling from underneath, your spangled bra top shows through, while the misty folds of your dress effectively hide any imperfections of the flesh.

The Compleat Belly Dancer
ABA*

the ethnic's bathrobe

This beautiful robe is often used by cabaret dancers as a comfortable cover-up in between performances. It can also be transformed into a traditional dance costume by catching a long scarf tightly about the hips. (Refer to illustration.)

THE VEIL*

About all you have to do to make a veil is to purchase a 2½–3-yard swath of soft fabric . . . chiffons, silks, nylons, rayons. It doesn't have to be expensive fabric . . . most veils can be purchased for less than $3.00. Finish the edges with the zigzag stitch on your machine, or make a neat narrow hem. You may add trim or sew on a few coins, but keep the adornments light in weight or your veil will fall awkwardly.

THE LADIES' HOME CABARET
changing your life

THE LADIES' HOME CABARET

Now that you're dancing, what . . . or where?

You've mastered a few swirls, gyrations, and even your Shimmy is getting nice and loose . . . so where do you go from here? Chances are, you're not interested in the life of a professional cabaret dancer. But now that you've put together a very original costume and know how to put it all together, the urge to share might lead you to consider giving a performance. Here are some suggestions as to where, how, and for whom.

Taxim section, in which the musici
play an improvisational solo. At this ti
your cymbals are still; you may be,
slowly, seductively yet modestly, rem
ing your veil, keeping your moveme
slow and sensuous. Sometimes the Tax
is brief, a mere prelude, and you will
have completed your veil removal. Do
rush . . . the veil work can well be
tended into the next part of the dan
slow but more rhythmic than the Tax

THE HOME CABARET

For an audience of one:

You've kept your practice sessions all between you and the mirror. Now you want to surprise your man. Serve him an exotic meal: shish kebab, rice pilaf, pita bread from the Armenian bakery, tart and tangy feta cheese (from goats . . . and Greece), followed by a baklava and Turkish coffee for dessert, and perhaps a snifter of Metaxa (Greek brandy). For the occasion, you've hung a canopy from the living-room ceiling, added a few Paisley print pillows, and lit some incense. You put on your dance record and bid your audience of one to make himself comfortable with his glass of ouzo (a licorice-tinged Greek liqueur) while you go change into your costume. With all the enthusiasm you can muster, you make your entrance. His initial shock will disappear as he senses how much fun you are having . . . and that this is all for him (tonight, anyway).

WHAT TO DO IF YOU GET COLD FEET RIGHT IN THE MIDDLE OF A SHIMMY: Just remember to keep your knees slightly bent, your eyes off your feet, and listen to the music. Act as if you are having the time of your life (I'm just showing you how much I love doing this, dear).

Use your veil to make a private canopy over his head . . . try to make HIM feel comfortable, and you will find yourself feeling completely sure of yourself and your Figure 8 sways.

For a party at your place:

Invite a few friends over . . . have them come in Oriental desert robes. Serve Middle Eastern foods. Keep the lights dim as your guests sprawl out on Oriental rugs and big fluffy pillows. Candlelight is great . . . lets you hide little mistakes in the mysterious shadows. (Be careful not to dance to close to the flame!)

Use lots of personality . . . eye contact, smiles. Walk around the pillow-strewn floor and do a little Shimmy for each guest.

Later, get everyone up to dance with you . . . start by soliciting the co-operation of one outgoing male guest. In the Middle East, couples belly dance together. Encourage others to join you . . . show them a simple hip circle and arm position.

When you are through dancing, slip an aba or hostess robe over your costume until you dry off. (Helps preserve the mystique of the costume also.)

You don't have to smile all the time . . . to do so would be to wear a frozen mask.

WHERE THE ETHNICS GO

An Old-World Family Gathering

Get yourself an invitation to an Armenian wedding celebration. Everyone will be dancing. You might end up doing a solo, though, and don't be surprised if gentlemen start throwing coins or dollar bills your way. It's an old, traditional, authentic, ethnic custom. It's also not considered out of line for a guest to insert a dollar bill in your clothing . . . such as a sleeve, belt, or necklace. Just smile and consider it a compliment. Should anyone get too transactional with his tip, wind up that electric Shimmy and dance your way out of it.

AN ETHNIC CABARET

If there's a Middle Eastern restaurant or night club in your city, pay a visit. Stick around till things get cozy and just get up and do a short simple dance. Make sure it's not the professional dancer's turn, though, and don't get too carried away with dramatic back bends and such.

In most cabarets, it is very common (and often encouraged) for members of the audience—male and female—to get up and dance.

Choose your clothes for the evening accordingly. No costumes, but a dress or pants outfit that makes movement easy . . . perhaps a scarf you can tie around your waist . . . and tuck your finger cymbals in your purse.

THE BOYS IN THE BAND

While you're in the club, pay attention to the musicians and their instruments. You'll see many kinds of instruments, depending on the club.

While you're in the club, pay attention to the musicians and their instruments. You'll see many kinds of instruments, depending on the club.

The Compleat Belly Dancer

Most typically, you'll find an oud and the drum. Other instruments might include the clarinet, violin, kanoon, bazooki . . . or an electric organ, electric guitar, and regular trap drums. Each band usually has one member who will sing as well as play his instrument. Some of the songs contain jokes, laments, stories, and emotional outcries. The dancer is a visual interpretation of the music. Watch and listen: Belly dancing is a multimedia happening.

Glossary

OUD DON'T SAY!
words and terms you'll be using

ABA (AH-bah) A loose-fitting, sometimes sheer, robe-dress of traditional origin. Also used as a dance costume, particularly for the more modest or sedate dancer. You can make one in an hour—see Chapter 6.

ALGIERS A North African nation in which belly dancing is popular.

ALLAH Arabic for God. Deity of the Moslem faith.

AYAWAH (EYE-a-wah) Arabic for "yes." Often murmured to a dancer.

BAZOOKI Stringed instrument first used only fifty years ago in Greece; now popular in the United States.

BELLY Round of the female abdomen; that area extending from the pelvic cradle to the cliff-edge of the rib cage. Preferably (in the eyes of the Middle East) a rather full, swelling curve or a mound of quivering

157

pillow-flesh. Includes womb, tummy, and abdominal muscles. Capable of hypnotic undulations and amazing rolls.

BELEDI (BEL-ah-dee) Literally translates as "native dance" . . . hence, it is correct to call the belly dance Beledi dancing. Also refers to traditional four-beat rhythm in lively part of the dance.

BERBERS North African tribes that centuries ago developed early abdominal movements in folk-culture dances. Women wore flowing indigo-dyed robes and prized amber jewelry by the pound.

BOLERO (bo-LEHR-oh) A slow, undulating Moorish rhythm, often associated with the slow, undulating belly-dance movements; also found in Spanish dancing influenced by Moors.

CABARET (ca-ber-AY) A traditional night club or *taverna* in which has developed a particular form of the traditional, ethnic belly dance. Also refers to type of costume worn therein.

CLARINET Often used in Middle Eastern musical combos; adds a plaintive "wailing" dimension; mostly used in Greek music.

CYMBALS Finger cymbals; silver-dollar-sized discs attached to the fingers, a pair on each hand, by elastic loops. Played throughout the belly-dance nation. Turkish women first used wooden spoons, two in each hand. Inspired the castanets of the Spanish dance.

DANCE Any movement or sequence of movements in which a feeling or attitude is expressed by—and transcends—the human body; what happens when the physical, emotional, spiritual, and mental centers are joined to manifest through the body form; to move rhythmically.

DANSA MORA Flamenco dance inspired by Moorish influence in Spain. Can be danced barefoot and utilizes finger cymbals.

DANSE DU VENTRE French description of the belly dance. Literally, "dance of the stomach." We were introduced to the form later, and translated it to belly. Anthropologists refer to it as abdominal dancing.

DEBKA (Also, DABKIE.) A Middle Eastern folk dance done in a lively line with a leader. (Loosely—it's walk-walk-walk-hop-step-hop, walk-walk-walk-hop-step-hop, etc.)

DEF Tambourine. Egyptian defs are beautifully inlaid with wood and mother of pearl.

DJELLABA The head covering or hooded robe worn by women in the Middle East.

DUMBEKI (Doom-BEHK-ee) (Also—dumbek or tamboura.) A pear-shaped or conical drum common to the Middle East. Made of metal or clay. Produces two basic sounds—a flat vibration (the dum) and a sharper, more metallic (tek).

EGYPT A North African country; part of the greater Arabic culture. Many authorities claim belly dancing had its earliest beginnings here. Egyptian dancing is subtle and exotic.

FALL Worn by belly dancers with short hair.

FEYROUZ The world-famous Arabic female singer. Also, a name borrowed by American cabaret belly dancers whose real names are Ann, Jane, or Gertrude.

KAFTAN Another loose traditional robe. Great for slipping in or out of. Easy to make for yourself or a man.

KANOON (kah-NOON) A zitherlike (like the auto-harp) instrument with movable bridges.

KEMANCHE (kah-MANCH-ah) A three-stringed violin-type instrument capable of producing ecstasy and near madness.

LEBANON An Arab state. Many famous cabarets for tourists in the city of Beirut.

MAQAM Arabic musical pattern, similar to the Indian "Raga."

MOROCCO Another belly-dance country, located in North Africa. Has great market places and bazaars. Visit the cabarets and see the boys doing the belly dancing. Scene of the annual week-long Marakesh Dance Festival which draws thousands of European and American tourists.

NEY A cane flute.

OPA! Greek exclamation . . . similar to Spanish *ole!*

OUD (OOD) Forerunner of the Elizabethan lute. An 11-stringed instrument with a round vault back. No frets. Lends itself miraculously to improvisation. Commonly played in city cabarets in its homelands—not a village instrument. Produces soulful, almost human sounds.

PERSIA Now is Iran. Ancient culture includes intricate dance movements and a classical form.

RABAB Fiddlelike instrument.

SAUDI ARABIA Another country in the Arab fertile crescent. Contains Mecca, holiest city of the Moslem faith; draws thousands of pilgrims each year. One who makes the pilgrimage is called, for the rest of his life, Hadji. (Remember Hadji Baba?)

SAZ A Turkish stringed instrument, similar to the bazooki, with a vault back, long skinny neck and quarter-tone fretting. Seven or nine strings, tuned in doubles or triples. A village instrument.

TAMBOURINE Percussion instrument consisting of a wooden ring affixed with metal cymbals. Played by gypsies throughout Middle East and Mediterranean. Adds a wild dimension to belly dancing. Often played by a member of the audience who wants to feel involved.

Glossary

TAXIM (tahks-EEM) Arabic for improvisation. The string player goes wild and free in a swirl of Middle Eastern soul. Inspires intense and dramatically prolonged dance movements.

TCHEFTETELLI Generally a slow, basic four-count rhythm, but watch out for the boys in the band—they'll speed it up if they feel so inclined.

TURKEY Located at mid-point between East and West; Istanbul, its largest and most important city, is half in Europe, half in Asia. Throughout time, the Turks have invaded and conquered much of the Middle Eastern and European worlds, and dispersed and assimilated various cultural traditions in the process. Some of the best folk dancing in the world is performed by Turkish exhibition troupes.

VEIL Traditionally worn by women of the Moslem world in compliance with religious codes and cultural dictates. Many countries now allow women to appear in public, daringly unveiled. Still a vital part of the belly dancer's costume.

YALA (YAH-lah) Arabic—means "come on!" as in *ole!* or *opa!*

YASU (YAH-sue) Greek for the exclamatory "yes." Often called out as a tribute to dancer, male or female.

ZAGHAREET (zie-ar-EET) Shrill warble issued as a re-action to music and dancing—similar to a repetitive Indian "war whoop."

ZILLS Ethnic term for finger cymbals.

Send for your copy of "The Compleat Belly Dancer" extended-play 45-rpm recording, created and specially written and arranged for readers of this book.

Send check or money order for $2.50 (includes shipping) to:

RIMAJA RECORDS
6200 Wilshire Boulevard
Suite 903
Los Angeles, California   90048

Be sure to include your name, address, city, state, and zip.

Finger cymbals ("Zills") are available through the same address at $4.50 a set (four antique-style imported cymbals with elastic finger loops).

160